D1234634

RULES THAT
BABIES LOOK BY
The Organization of Newborn Visual Activity

RULES THAT
BABIES LOOK BY
The Organization of Newborn Visual Activity

MARSHALL M. HAITH
University of Denver

LEA LAWRENCE ERLBAUM ASSOCIATES, PUBLISHERS
1980   Hillsdale, New Jersey

Lawrence Erlbaum Associates, Inc., Publishers
365 Broadway
Hillsdale, New Jersey 07642

Library of Congress Cataloging in Publication Data

Haith, Marshall M. 1937–
    Rules that newborn babies look by.

    Bibliography: p.
    Includes index.
    1. Visual perception in children.   2. Cognition in children.   3. Infant psychology.   4. Infants
(Newborn)   I. Title.
BF720.V57H34   155.4'22   80–10601
ISBN 0-89859-033-7

Printed in the United States of America

Dedicated to my family,
Mom, Dad, Sue, Mike, Brian, and Gary

Contents

Preface

This book describes a new approach to an old question. The question concerns what abilities the newborn human possesses to take on the task of learning about the world. The approach involves both a conceptual and a methodological redirection. A full exposition of these themes takes some time and, in a sense, occupies the full book. However, some introductory remarks will give the flavor of what follows.

Let me begin by saying I limit myself in this book to a discussion of the newborn's visual world. Speculation about newborn vision (by newborn I mean the first several days—usually 7—of life) can be found in the earliest writings of the "fathers" of modern psychology (for example, see Helmholtz, 1894, in Warren & Warren, 1968; James, 1890). Generally, the newborn's visual world was thought to be a mass of confusion and his ability to deal with it limited to a few simple reflexes. Desirous of moving beyond speculation, investigators in subsequent decades invented a number of impressive methodological approaches and technologies for visual research with infants. As a consequence of these advances and theoretical work, the general conceptions of early infancy have undergone several reorientations. In the first phase, during the early decades of the 1900s, the principal concern was with visual reflexes, such as pupillary constriction and dilation, or with the changes in visual stimuli that produced a response, such as brightness, color, and movement. Here, the baby was seen as a passive and reflexive recipient of stimuli and the question was "What can the young infant sense"?

After studies were performed at the University of Iowa in the 1930s that were concerned with the effect of light level on general activity, there was relative disinterest in newborn and early-infant vision until the 1950s and early 1960s when psychology witnessed a renaissance of sorts, a "paradigm shift," that produced a new characterization of man and his infancy as that of seeker of information rather than of Pavlovian-Thorndikian collator of stimulus events. Fantz's suggestion of a paradigm for studying infant attention meshed neatly with the zeitgeist and profoundly affected the direction of infant research. The question of the pre-1960s changed from "What stimuli does the newborn sense?" to that in the post-1960s, "What information does the newborn attend to or prefer?"

Presumably the infant was now seen to be more active and dynamic than before, capable of selecting input, no longer a slave to the stimulus world. I say "presumably" because careful analysis of the research questions asked and the prototheories developed indicates that the infant is considered to be less "dynamic" and "active" than casual discussion suggests. The baby is currently characterized as a multiple-choice decision operator who surveys the visual field and decides to look at one stimulus instead of another (or others).

With this conceptualization of the infant, the goal had become to discover the characteristics of a stimulus, or more accurately, the dimensions and levels of dimensions of stimuli that controlled the baby's selective attention. Thus the notion of the infant as a "dynamic" and "active" governor of his/her own stimulus-seeking activity became essentially an articulation of the standard learning-theory distinction between "potential" and "effective" stimuli. (The term "potential stimuli" refers to all stimuli in the field, whereas "effective stimuli" are those that gain control over behavior because the organism orients itself toward them.) Of course, learning theory was concerned with articulating postreception functions for effective stimuli, whereas attention theory has been concerned with spelling out why stimuli are effective in the first place. But the major point is that investigators have been concerned principally with stimulus analysis even though lip service is paid to the importance of considering the "dynamic" and "active" aspects of the infant.

We are left with the same problem as we were before we distinguished effective from potential stimuli; i.e., what is the organism doing with the effective stimuli? Detailed analysis of infant visual activity, even newborn activity, reveals that the eyes move at least every half second more than 90% of the time. Measures of the total amount of time a baby looks at a stimulus pattern or the duration of the infant's first look at it, by far the most common measures in the field, hardly capture the "dynamic" aspects of the visual-processing activity. Nor are they likely to tell us about general principles by which the system operates. These measures can inform us about stimuli a baby senses, but they can not tell us how the baby is organized to acquire information about the visual world.

I argue that the current stimulus-oriented approaches to understanding infant visual activity are conceptually misleading, especially for the newborn.

A more satisfactory point of view, and one that accommodates current beliefs about the baby's role in gathering information from the world, emphasizes the organization of visual activity itself and the principles by which it operates. These are my concerns in this book. I assume that there is meaningful structure in the newborn's activity and that careful description, analysis, and interpretation of this structure are required for an adequate articulation of the baby's competencies.

Heretofore investigations have assumed that an adequate theory of infant visual activity would result from an analysis of the structure of the environment and, perhaps, a catalogue of the infant's experience with the visual world. Of course, the baby does behave in a context, so visual circumstances must be considered. But an emphasis on structure in behavior rather than on stimulus structure yields different questions from the standard tack. In taking the perspective of the organism, one is prompted to ask questions about how information seeking is adapted to cope with various visual circumstances rather than how stimulus dimensions govern responses. This is more than semantic permutation as the change in emphasis has direct research consequences. Standard approaches constrain their measures of behavior, leaving the degrees of freedom for variation in the stimulus. The approach I have used is to constrain the stimulus situation and leave the behavior free to vary as it is carefully observed.

I make the basic assumption that, from birth, the infant has organized ways of dealing with different visual circumstances. I characterize the dispositions the newborn possesses for dealing with these visual circumstances as "rules." One could argue that the search for rules of visual scanning in newborns is a "test by fire" for the conception that infant visual activity is organized for information gathering. The newborn, generally held to be a decorticate organism, would be most likely of all-age infants to abide by the notion (still popular in some circles) that early infancy is a period of one-shot reflexive responding to stimuli, as opposed to a notion that emphasizes continuous activity that is adapted to the visual world. Indeed, it has been claimed that early infancy is the time when the baby is "captured by stimuli," as opposed to his older counterpart who presumably "captures stimuli."

On the other hand, from an adaptational perspective one might suspect that newborn infants, more so than older infants, would obey a fairly constrained biologically based set of instructions or rules for seeking visual information. By this hypothesis the newborn would be an ideal candidate for discovering such rules. At this early time, rules that govern visual activity might, in part, serve to "get the newborn going" on the task of learning about the visual world—a problem totally unexplored in theories of perceptual development and really unmanageable by reflex or preference theories. I propose a set of ideas and studies that will throw light on how the newborn "gets going" and, perhaps, a more fruitful way of thinking about how the infant "keeps going."

I wrote this book principally with the graduate student of psychology and the professional academic/researcher psychologist in mind. This group of readers will probably want to read all the sections of the book except, perhaps, for some of the more detailed discussion of method and procedures that is provided in Chapter 2; I advise the reader who simply wishes an overview of procedures to skip to the summary section at the end of this chapter.

I feel that other readers can also benefit from reading this book. Neonatologists, pediatricians, nurses, and others who are interested in early behavior should find several of the sections of the book to be of interest, especially the portions that contrast my general perspective of the infant with more popular perspectives. These readers may wish to read summaries of the results sections of Chapters 3–7 rather than to work through all the statistical approaches that were used. For these readers, I have provided a summary paragraph at the beginning of each results section; the reader may then turn immediately to the discussion section of the chapter without losing the continuity of the presentation. Finally, after reading the method section of Chapter 3, readers who are less interested in the procedural details of each study should be able to skip the methods section of Chapters 4–7 and still be able to understand the major findings of each study.

Other chapters should be read in toto with, perhaps, one exception. Two sections of Chapter 9 require knowledge of neurophysiology and may be too difficult for some readers. At the minimum, however, the chapter should be skimmed, as the groundwork for Chapter 10 is established here.

Many people have contributed to the research, methods, and conceptions I describe. This work was carried out at the Cambridge Hospital, Cambridge, Massachusetts, while I was at Harvard University serving as an Assistant Professor and Lecturer from 1966-1972. However, the technology was acquired in large part at Yale University, and the conceptualizations grew naturally from those developed during two postdoctoral years I spent there working with William Kessen, Phil Salapatek, and Arnold Sameroff. Additionally, my ideas have been affected during my years (since 1972) at the University of Denver. My work, therefore, reflects the influence of innumerable graduate students and colleagues that I have known during my full professional career, and I have been blessed with the best. I want to thank the staff and administration of the Cambridge Hospital for providing space and facilities for this work. Dr. Phil Porter, Chief of Pediatrics, and Ms. Mildred Howard, Head Nurse, were especially supportive. Robert Lentz made invaluable contributions to technological development. Henry Gerbrands and Fred Morrison helped in the early stages of setting up laboratories. Tina Turner, Gail Brent, Diane Lusk, Joy Corsi, Terry Bergman, Leah Mann, Morton Mendelson, and Karen Cohen all helped in the running of subjects and/or the reduction of data. Many of these people have also helped in the development of my thinking, and I also owe thanks to Jerome Kagan, William Kessen, Phil Salapatek, and Arnold Sameroff for their counsel over the years as this research developed. Morton Mendelson commented on several versions of this manuscript and made many helpful suggestions. Finally, I am grateful to Betty Richardson for her help in preparing the manuscript and for her substantive suggestions.

The research reported here was supported by National Institute of Mental health grants MH22020 and MH23412. Without generous support from NIMH, the work included here would have been impossible. I would also like to acknowledge the John Simon Guggenheim Memorial Foundation for their fellowship support of my sabbatical year in Paris, 1978–1979, during which time I completed the final revisions of this book.

I dedicated this book to my family for good reason. My mom and dad, Frances and Nathan Haith, have provided lifelong encouragement and support for my work. I am thankful to my patient and understanding wife, Sue, who has tolerated the indulgences of an academic researcher, and to my boys, Mike, Brian, and Gary, who have served in my experiments and stimulated my ideas through their own development.

Marshall M. Haith

1
Introduction

Research on infant perception and attention has flourished since around 1960 when behavioristic learning theory lost its privileged status as the dominant theoretical system in psychology.The change of mood is reflected in several books (for example, Bruner, Goodnow, & Austin, 1956; Miller, Galanter, & Pribram, 1960) that indicated a renewed interest of psychologists in internal processes that mediate experience. Berlyne's *Conflict, Arousal, and Curiosity* (1960) was especially important for the relatively inactive field of infancy. The new trend fostered a shift from an almost exclusive interest in biological functions to an interest in perceptual and cognitive processes. The simple but profound question has been, what is the nature of the infant's visual world and what are the changes that occur on the way to adulthood?

Psychologists interested in infancy quickly appreciated the potential importance of attentional concepts for understanding visual behavior. However, an adequate methodology was lacking until Fantz (1958, 1961) popularized an easily implemented technique which opened new vistas in infant visual research. Indeed, the studies of infant vision since 1960 that have used the Fantz technique, numbering into the several hundreds, stand as dramatic testimony to the impact of his contribution (see Bond, 1972; Cohen & Salapatek, 1975; Haith & Campos, 1977; Hershenson, 1970; Horowitz, 1968; and Kessen, Haith, & Salapatek, 1970, for general reviews).

Fantz (1958, 1961) suggested that a very straightforward technique can be used to study a baby's attention to a visual stimulus. A person can determine what a baby attends by watching the baby's eyes! The reflection of the

1

stimulus the baby fixates appears on the cornea near the center of the black pupillary opening of the eye.

Typically, the infant is given an opportunity to look at two visual stimuli that are presented simultaneously while an observer watches his eyes. The observer notes which of the two stimuli is fixated first and for how long. The stimulus that is viewed first, the greatest number of times, and/or longest is said to be preferred and selectively attended by the baby. A variant of this procedure employs stimuli presented singly, in sequence; relative "preference" is then determined by how long each stimulus is fixated in comparison to all stimuli in the set.

The Fantz paradigm has been unmatched for utility and applicability to a wide range of issues and problems in infancy including: attention, habituation, learning, cognition, preference, detection, discrimination, recognition, identification, intermodal and space perception, motivation and affect. The ocular-orientation measure has been especially useful as an indicator of perceptual sensitivity (or discrimination). We know from these studies and studies carried out earlier that newborns and young infants are sensitive to several physical visual dimensions—light (Blanton, 1917; Pratt, Nelson, & Sun, 1930), brightness of light (Doris, Casper, & Poresky, 1967; Hershenson, 1964), movement (Dayton, Jones, Steele, & Rose, 1964b; Haith, 1966), and possibly color (Barnet, Lodge, & Armington, 1965; Chase, 1937). And it is reasonably well agreed that, even at birth, infants respond to pattern (Fantz, 1958, 1965; Stirnimann, 1944).

Unfortunately, the great popularity of the Fantz paradigm and its broad applicability have produced conceptual problems. As might be expected in a field that lay dormant for so long and then blossomed dramatically, there were early growing pains. So little empirical information existed initially that the collection of almost any kind of attentional-preference data was greeted with enthusiasm. Stimulus choices for experiments often appeared to be unmotivated by any theoretical concerns with the result that many of the findings are difficult to organize conceptually.

A similar problem seems attributable to the range of applicability of this paradigm. Often, investigators have tied the discussion of their results to other studies that used similar paradigms rather than to a literature which posed the same questions. Although the introduction to a report may claim that perceptual discrimination is under investigation, considerations about stimulus preference, stimulus habituation, attention, cognitive development, and even the paradigm itself often creep into the discussion. This is no problem if a unifying conceptualization exists which accommodates these processes. But it does not exist. And the result has been some confusion over exactly what issue a set of findings is relevant to. I pursue this matter more extensively in the following.

For the present discussion I am concerned with conceptualizations about what factors control infant visual attention. By far the greatest number of studies bear on this question, and these conceptualizations constitute one perspective on how the baby learns about the visual world. Four major conceptual and research trends have focused on understanding what controls attention as infants develop—complexity theory, discrepancy theory, novelty theory, and the ethological position.

CURRENT THEORIES OF VISUAL ACTIVITY

Complexity Theory.   Several studies followed the suggestion of Dember and Earl (1957) and Berlyne (1960) that attentional preference of organisms for stimuli depends on the relation between the informational complexity of the stimulus and the processing capabilities of the organism. Stimuli can be seen as containing a certain amount of information (complexity), presumably quantifiable in information-theory terms. Their presence provides a given information-flow rate for the infant. An infant can be characterized as having a particular adaptation level for rate of information flow. This organismic level determines the level of complexity the infant prefers; presumably, the infant prefers a level that is just beyond the baby's current processing capabilities, which the baby then "processes," resulting in an increment in adaptation level. The implication for a theory of development is clear. Development consists of continual increments in the complexity of the individual as a result of interaction with "pacer" stimuli. Each increment further increases the informational level or stimulus complexity the subject can manage.

Notice that complexity theory is, in fact, a motivational theory. Although this assertion seems fairly straightforward, the discussions of complexity as an important stimulus dimension have typically focused on perceptual and cognitive-attentional issues, whereas the motivational concerns have been virtually ignored.

Some investigators have found evidence of stimulus preference that correlates with their interpretation of complexity (Berlyne, 1958; Brennan, Ames, & Moore, 1966; Cohen, 1969; Hershenson, 1964; Hershenson, Munsinger, & Kessen, 1965; Thomas, 1965), and others have even found preference for increasing complexity with age (Brennan et al., 1966). But on the whole, the concept of complexity has not been fruitful. Definitions have differed strikingly from one study to the next (McCall & Melson, 1970) and physical parameters of the patterned stimuli that have been used (mostly checkerboards)—such as area of the figure, length of contour, angularity, and brightness—have sometimes been hopelessly confounded with manipulations of "complexity" (Karmel, 1969; McCall & Melson, 1970), as has the size and number of elements (Fantz, Fagan, & Miranda, 1975). Additionally, age functions have not been easily replicated; an untangling of the stimulus factors has revealed amount or average length of contour in a stimulus to be more critical in attracting the infant's gaze than complexity (Karmel & Maisel, 1975). One problem in varying the complexity of visual forms and giving the infant free viewing opportunity is that there is no control over the sequence with which higher or lower complexity portions of the form are taken in or whether, in fact, the whole form is inspected. To sidestep these problems, Haith, Kessen, and Collins (1969) manipulated complexity in sequentially-presented stimuli by varying the predictability with which lights flashed. Predictability is an agreed upon interpretation of complexity. A response function was found which was precisely opposite to predictions from complexity theory. Thus, complexity theory has not fared well. However, the relative amount of contour in a stimulus does affect the duration of looking (McCall & Melson, 1970; Karmel & Maisel, 1975).

Discrepancy Theory. A second theoretical position relates infants' preferences for visual stimuli to memory representations of stimulus classes. It is argued that the infant attempts to "match" say, a face, to a cognitive schema that the baby has for faces from previous experience (Kagan, 1970; Lewis, 1969). The infant attends to stimuli that are "optimally discrepant" from a schema the infant possesses, because he/she must exert cognitive effort to assimilate the stimulus to the schema. If a stimulus is too familiar it will be easily assimilated and, thus, not attended very long. If it is too discrepant, it will be ignored. In fairness, it should be pointed out that Kagan believes that discrepancy from a schema is an effective principle in controlling attention only after 2 months of age. He feels that physical parameters such as brightness, color, and movement control attention before then, and he adopts the rule system I describe later to account for very early infant attention. Still, it is useful to consider discrepancy theory as it is the dominant position in the field, and an understanding of conceptualizations of visual activity at 2 months might help us to think about visual activity from birth on.

In the standard paradigm, the infant is shown a variety of stimuli that fall on a presumed dimension of discrepancy from a schema; for example, if the face schema were under study, a picture of a schematic face, one of a face with the internal features reassembled and one with those features missing, might be shown to a baby under the prediction that the "face" that is optimally discrepant would be fixated most (Kagan, 1970). Unfortunately, it is not possible to specify, a priori, at what stage the infant's schema is in—even an outline drawing of a two-dimensional face must be somewhat discrepant for an infant from the infant's experience with real faces—and the ordering of stimuli along a discrepancy dimension is often questionable. Although post hoc interpretation of results by this framework have seemed intuitively satisfying, the danger of circularity is obvious. Additionally, one must assume that the infant tries to assimilate the presented stimulus to the same schema that the experimenter has in mind.

An improvement on this paradigm establishes the schema experimentally by familiarizing the baby with one stimulus and then presenting alternatives that vary incrementally from the standard along one or two physical dimensions; here, the schema is presumably known as is the discrepancy ordering of the alternatives. An extreme discrepancy is also included which varies multidimensionally from all the other stimuli. Results from one study showed a correlated increase in preference with increments in discrepancy (Zelazo, Hopkins, Jacobson, & Kagan, 1974); however, the predicted decline in preference only occurred for the extreme variation. A criticism of this study is that there is no assurance the baby was comparing the extreme variation to the same schema used for the other alternatives; since no independent evaluation was made of how attractive the extreme variant was, the results may only indicate that it was simply less attractive than the other alternatives. Unless a decline in preference can be demonstrated at extreme discrepancy levels along a known dimension, results can be accounted for by a simpler, novelty interpretation.

A recent article by McCall, Kennedy, and Appelbaum (1977) goes a long way toward meeting earlier experimental criticisms. They used well-specified stimulus dimensions and varied the "schema-setting" and comparison stimuli across infant groups with two quite different sets of stimuli. Babies' looking time supported the curvilinear predictions of discrepancy theory. These authors also martialed a substantial amount of other evidence in support of the notion that looking time is, indeed, related by a curvilinear function to stimulus discrepancy.

Still, we have no assurance that the habituating stimuli and the most discrepant stimuli, to which the babies looked least during recovery trials, were really seen as most dissimilar among those items of the stimulus set. A convincing demonstration would show that even though the most discrepant stimulus is more easily discriminated from the standard than the intermediate discrepancy stimuli, it still produces less looking than the intermediate exemplars.

One advantage of discrepancy theory is that provision has been made for different determinants of "attention" as the infant develops through the first year of life (Kagan, 1970). Infants are in a prediscrepancy phase prior to 2 months of age, at which time they enter a discrepancy phase, and, finally, in the last third of their first year of life, a hypothesis-construction phase. Looking time is held to be related to babies' behavior in each of these phases. No other attention theory has as well-articulated a developmental scheme as discrepancy theory.

Yet, there are several conceptual questions that still prove troublesome. Theorists have ignored the problem of how a new schema is established; logically, a newborn should have no schemas and should never develop any because totally new stimuli should be ignored. Questions like these arise naturally from consideration of the theory as it is stated, even though they may seem inappropriate for a conceptualization that purports to explain attention: here is the crux of much confusion in the field.

Careful examination of Kagan's work and that of his colleagues reveals that discrepancy theory is not really concerned with explaining attention or its determinants as has been claimed; rather, investigators use duration of looking, usually called "attention," to explore early cognitive development. "Attention" (really receptor orientation) is simply treated as an indicator of cognitive activity—effort expended toward assimilating the stimulus to a schema.

An appreciation of this distinction is useful as it implies no necessary conflict between Kagan's theory and anyone else's. Stimuli may be attractive because of certain perceptual parameters such as novelty, color, movement, amount of contour, or because the infant is engaged in cognitive efforts to assimilate them. These factors presumably could operate cooperatively or antagonistically depending on the strength of the physical parameters and the infant's experience. However, an appreciation of this distinction leads one to ask such questions about discrepancy theory as what the principle is for establishing a new schema, how intraschema stimuli are differentiated, how schemas are interrelated, what the transition rules are by which the baby moves from prediscrepancy to discrepancy functioning, and so on—in short, questions that would naturally be asked about a theory of *cognitive* development. These questions have not been addressed. Thus, although discrepancy theory has substantial intuitive appeal and has generated a great deal of research, it remains incomplete as a cognitive theory, for which "attention" is used as an index, and inappropriate as a theory of attention. An additional factor to consider is that discrepancy theory contains no motivational component, placing it somewhat outside the context of complexity theory to which it has often been opposed. Essentially, motivation is created, according to discrepancy theory, by a discrepant stimulus. When a discrepant stimulus is encountered, the baby is energized to assimilate it into a schema. But how do we account for a baby's visual activity when no discrepant stimulus is present? Whereas complexity theory contains the notion that optimal complexity stimuli are reinforcing, and are sought out when the information-flow rate provided by available stimuli declines below the adaptation level, discrepancy theory contains no such feature. "Discrepant" stimuli are not sought out.

Both theories, however, deal with the developmental issue. Babies become continually more complex as they encounter increasingly complex stimuli, which, in turn, advances their adaptation level. Or, babies' schemas become continually inclusive as they accommodate to an increasingly broad range of stimuli.

Novelty Theory.   A third position, not really identifiable with any one individual except perhaps Berlyne (1960), is that novelty is the key principle governing attention. Many studies have documented the importance of novelty for infants over 2 months of age. However, most of these studies were principally concerned with the process of habituation and used novel stimuli primarily to demonstrate that the infant's visual interest would recover to a nonhabituated stimulus. As a consequence, stimuli have not usually been selected to elaborate particular aspects of novelty theory, and it is the least developed of the various positions. Still, several theorists believe that stimulus novelty and habituation to stimulus novelty work together to shape early visual development. Sokolov (1960) is frequently cited as having laid down the basic elements of this position. Essentially, a novel stimulus produces an orienting response (similar to the kind of response Pavlov referred to as a "What is it?" response). As this stimulus is repeatedly presented, an internal model of that stimulus is created. When this model is completed, habituation occurs and the subject no longer responds to the stimulus. It is unclear whether each stimulus has its own model or whether stimulus classes are constructed. Also, there is no complete specification of the principles by which some stimuli are protected from habituation, such as those associated with food.

Novelty theory, as with complexity and discrepancy theory, does contain the seeds of an explanation of visual development. As more novel stimuli are encourntered, more cognitive models are created. However, novelty theory contains no motivational principle or principle to get the baby going. Rather, a novel stimulus is presented and responded to or not, depending on whether an adequate cognitive model has been built.

An interesting subissue, within the context of novelty theory, has appeared in the literature which deserves comment. An early study by Fantz (1964) indicated that infants under 2 months of age could not habituate to a repeated stimulus. This finding was upheld by a number of studies (for example, Clifton, 1968; Haith, 1966). Although investigators were most interested in this phenomenon for what it implied about lack of memory capability in the first 2 months, the finding also had an interesting implication for the capacity of novelty theory to explain early visual behavior. If a baby could not habituate to a stimulus, then either no stimulus or all stimuli would be novel; whichever the case, principles of novelty could not be used to explain early-infant behavior. Although this problem was generally overlooked, the issue is moot now because several studies have reported habituation even in newborns, with specially adapted procedures (for example, Friedman, 1972; Friedman, Bruno, & Vietze, 1974; Paden, 1975).

It is clear that babies beyond 2 months do habituate, (see Paden, 1975, for a qualification) *generally* faster than younger infants. It appears, then, that there is an age-related change, either in the attractiveness of novel stimuli or in the rate with which babies become bored with old stimuli.

Ethological Position.　Finally, there is what may best be described as an ethologically oriented position for understanding infant attention. It is held that through evolution, selection pressures have favored organisms who attend to features of the environment that have adaptive significance for them. Fantz (1961) held this position early in his writings but has moved more closely to a position favoring complexity as the important dimension of stimulation (Fantz & Nevis, 1967) or a position that concentrates on particular physical features of stimuli (Fantz et al., 1975). Much of the research on faces has turned on whether a picture of a "face" is preferred over other patterned stimuli, because the configuration of a face is an ethologically meaningful triggering stimulus or because it attracts attention through such physical characteristics as symmetry. Studies of infants younger than 5 months of age have produced contradictory results (Haaf & Bell, 1967; Wilcox, 1969). There is general agreement that pictures of faces are not preferred over other stimuli, equated for contrast and number of elements, until about 4 months of age.

An ethologically oriented approach to the problem of what governs infant visual activity has several failings. One failing it shares with discrepancy and novelty theory is that there is no principle for dealing with the baby's activity in the absence of "ethologically relevant" stimuli. A second failing is that there is no provision for development. Ethological approaches tend to describe stimulus-behavior relations in a one-shot fashion that deny developmental plasticity.

It should be clear from this brief review that there is anything but consensus on what controls attention. Some of the difficulty stems from an inability to determine what the infant is responding to. For example, the theoretical positions described make the tacit assumption that presented stimulus configurations are seen by infants at all ages as a whole. Common sense and data (Salapatek, 1968; Salapatek & Kessen, 1966) render this a dubious assumption at best. A few investigations have recently attempted more rigorous control over stimuli to determine what specifically is attracting infant gaze (Fantz et al., 1975; Karmel, 1969; McCall & Melson, 1970; Moffett, 1969; Pipp, 1978; Ruff & Birch, 1974). An additional problem is definitional. How complexity, discrepancy, novelty, and ethological "value" are defined is often debatable. Still a third problem revolves around the interpretation that investigators have given to the construct, "attention." James (1890) used "attention" to refer to a filtering process, an internal delimiting of the range of stimuli available to the receptors (or stimuli available from memory), similar to the way Broadbent (1952, 1958) has interpreted it. But most in the infant-research tradition have used "attention" simply to refer to receptor orientation; "attention" here means "looking at," which is closer to Wyckoff's (1952) interpretation in delineating potential and effective stimuli for learning theory. Still a third use refers to intensive rather than selective activity; that is, how much "attention" is given to a stimulus? Or how activated is a baby when a stimulus appears? Or how long or slowly does looking decline? This latter interpretation is closer to that used by Duffy (1957) in activation theory and by Sharpless and Jasper (1956) in their work on habituation.

Investigators have ranged broadly in their usage of "attention." Most frustrating is their conceptual use of one interpretation, usually the James-Broadbent version, and their empirical use of a second interpretation, that of receptor orientation. To make matters even more complicated, these two uses are sometimes mixed with an attempt to use receptor orientation as an indicator of still another, cognitive, process.

Aside from all of these specific concerns, I think it is fair to step back and ask whether conceptual flaws in the theories, definitional issues, and infirming data are really the principal concerns. I think not. The important issue is whether the right question has been asked, and again, I would respond negatively. I believe it is not being asked because investigators have accepted an implicit view of the young infant that is off the mark.

Let us take stock of what I have been doing in the last several pages. I was considering explanations of why an infant prefers to look at some stimuli more than others. These explanations appealed to relations between levels along a stimulus dimension and a level of the baby, along a related parameter, to account for the preference. Three "high-level" assumptions, in common, are made by these approaches:

1. The baby can be thought of as a creature who inventories the visual field and chooses to look at or attend to some things more than others.

2. The impetus for visual behavior lies in the stimulus.

3. The organizational principles for visual behavior are to be found in stimuli.

ASSUMPTIONS OF CURRENT THEORIES

The Baby as a Creature of Preference.   Current conceptualizations characterize the baby as a multiple-choice, decision-making device that surveys the field and, then, on the basis of some dimension that relates the alternatives, chooses a stimulus that is "just right" on that dimension. After habituating or assimilating or adapting to that stimulus, the infant chooses a second one to look at and so on. The evolution of this conception of the infant was quite natural given the wide acceptance of the attention paradigm. The

Fantz looking technique is ideal for studies of stimulus preference. From a totally nontheoretical start, investigators soon began to develop conceptualizations to account for babies' behavior *in this paradigm*. It was not a far leap to begin to think of the baby in his/her world in terms of a generalization from the laboratory setting.

Although a natural development, one should ask about the validity of a conceptualization of an organism that depends so heavily on the paradigm used to study it. There is a clear analogue to the sequellae psychology experienced in the heyday of behavior theory. At first, the operant response box was seen to be a convenient tool to study learning. Soon, theories were developed to account for behavior in such boxes and, not long after, organisms' worlds were conceptualized as an elaborated version of such a box and their behavior as a generalization of their operant-box performance. In brief, rather than the conceptualization giving birth to the paradigm, the paradigm captured the conceptualization. Casual observation of even an awake newborn infant produces an impression that contrasts sharply with the robot-like quality of visual behavior that we are led to expect from current attention theories.

From my own research (to be reported) and that of others (Kessen, Salapatek, & Haith, 1972; Salapatek & Kessen, 1966), babies have been found to move their eyes at least twice each second 90% of the time. It is true, by mechanical necessity, that the fovea of the eyes can only be directed toward one tiny area at a time as the eyes fixate and move, fixate and move.[1] However, we would probably not want to claim that each 1/3 to 1/2 second fixation represents a "preference" of the baby for the fixated area over all other areas. In fact, investigators have typically talked about degree of attention or preference for the whole stimulus, as they define it. Still, given the information that babies are continuously visually active, the measures that investigators have used—duration of looking at a stimulus—must really reflect many fixations on that stimulus. A careful description of what the baby is doing, then, must involve a notion of scanning rather than simply looking. This consideration raises suspicions about the adequacy of a preference vocabulary to deal with the baby's visual activity.

"Adequacy," of course, depends on one's perspective. If the baby is seen as a preference creature, and the task is to describe his stimulus-preference hierarchy and each dimension-preference function, then a preference vocabulary is adequate as is the looking-duration measure. Thomas (1973), for example, captured the prevalent conception in a recent statement: "The author has long believed that an understanding of the infant's responses to visual

---

[1] For the sake of clarity, I am ignoring here the question of whether the baby can process much of the peripheral field of view. Generally, I sidestep this question and assume that the baby fixates the general area currently being processed.

stimuli could best be approached through a theory of choice. Thus, the position taken here is that the baby's looking behavior belongs to a theory of preferential choice behavior [p. 468]." However, I believe that the important information is what a baby is doing or trying to do with his/her visual array, not how long the baby does it.

Still other inadequacies in the traditional explanations become evident when other aspects of the baby's visual activity are considered. A glance at publications in the field indicates that in a typical preference study with a fixed stimulus-presentation period, babies spend about one-half the time looking at the stimuli. Further, the nonpreferred stimulus may be looked at perhaps only 5%–10% less than the preferred stimulus. It is reasonable to ask why the baby only looks at the stimuli 50% of the time and what the baby is up to when not looking at the experimenter's stimuli. And, what is the baby doing with the *non*preferred stimuli? These questions arise if one is concerned with an adequate account of infant visual behavior as opposed to how babies perform in two-choice visual-preference situations.

I want to be clear about my concerns. There is nothing wrong at all with the Fantz preference paradigm. In fact, it has been tremendously valuable for studying a number of processes, and it will continue to be. Obviously, a paradigm is neither good nor bad. What I object to is the assumption that it is useful to think of the young infant, generally, as a creature of choice or preference. Proposed theories probably do an adequate job of accounting for visual behavior in simple two-choice situations. But I believe that the notion of the infant as a choice creature has no more heuristic value than thinking of the adult as a preference creature and trying to build a complete under-standing of the adult's visual behavior on the basis of the individual's two-choice behavior. Thus, I believe assumption (1), that babies can be thought of as creatures of preference, is faulty and limiting. Now, let us consider the assumption concerning the impetus for visual behavior.

The Impetus for Visual Behavior.   Although theorists have not directly discussed the impetus for visual behavior in very young infants, implicit in their descriptions is the notion that stimuli "drive" visual activity. Looking activity results from comparisons of stimuli along a dimension. As men-tioned earlier, this assumption faces problems when the infant has no "optimal" stimuli around, as is usually the case when the infant is in the very familiar surrounding of home, room, and crib. If no stimuli are available, as in darkness, or in a homogeneous field, visual activity would be expected to stop. As we see in a later discussion, babies' actual behavior does not conform to this expectation.

I describe a way of thinking about visual activity that assumes that visual behavior is ongoing. Stimuli, by this notion, do not produce behavior, they actually constrain it. The baby can be seen as pursuing an "agenda," biologically given. To the extent that scanning of the available visual stimuli facilitates the accomplishment of this "agenda," visual scanning activity is constrained in particular ways. The notion that stimuli constrain rather than produce visual activity is helpful in talking about visual activity both conceptually and empirically. Visual behavior in the absence of stimuli can be accommodated and the interrelation between the natural "baseline" activity of the dynamic biological visual system and the effect of environmental input can be addressed. At the empirical level, "noise" in visual fixations (that is, nonstimulus fixations) can be understood as part of the natural system activity that the stimulus has not constrained. Under this notion of stimulus constraint, the ultimate goal shifts from attempting to explain each eye movement and fixation in cause-effect, stimulus-response fashion to attempting to understand how parameters of scanning (scanning range, size of movement, etc.) are altered by various visual arrays and why. These considerations lead to questions about the organizing principles of visual behavior.

The Organizing Principles for Visual Behavior.   Current theories assume that the organizing principles for visual behavior can be best understood from a stimulus-dimension perspective. Although the baby's "level," relevant to the hypothesized dimension, has been considered, the hypothetical consequences of the baby finding a stimulus which lies at varying distances from the optimum are internal; they have no particular effects on visual behavior other than to affect looking duration. The obsession with the summary looking-duration measure has, in fact, discouraged attempts to seek organization in visual behavior and, in the absence of a perspective which assumes that organization exists in the more detailed aspects of visual activity, there has been little reason for investigators to try to overcome the methodological difficulties involved in more analytic work. Actually, three factors have guided psychologists away from considering organization in visual behavior. The first of these is conceptual: investigators believe the baby can be thought of as a preference creature and that the organizing factors that control the behavior they have been interested in—looking duration—can be found in stimulus dimensions. Second, the ease with which the looking-duration measure could be used guided investigators away from studying more detailed visual activity. Relatedly and finally, the advanced technology required to do precise eye-fixation research on young infants has served as a deterrent.

In the pages that follow I describe a method and several studies that have shaped my view of the most appropriate way to think about infant visual activity. First, I describe the method (Chapter 2) and five studies that were carried out with newborn babies (Chapters 3-7). Then, I summarize the major findings and conclusions and present a different way of thinking about early-infant visual behavior, in terms of a rule system the newborn possesses for acting on the visual world (Chapter 8). Chapter 9 summarizes early-infant visual competencies and proposes that one overriding *organismic* principle governs visual activity in the early weeks—to maximize cortical-firing rate. Documentation of the operation of this principle is provided through a discussion of known facts of human and subhuman neurophysiology. Chapter 10 provides a synthesis of the behavioral and neurophysiological facts, and Chapter 11 offers some clarifications amd disclaimers.

What I conclude is that early visual activity can not be understood in terms of infant reflexes, infant preference, or in terms of stimulus organization alone. The newborn must be thought of as a biologically organized creature who behaves visually in a continuous rather than in a discrete preferential or attentional fashion. The "agenda" that nature has established for the newborn must be considered as well as the infant's organization for accomplishing that agenda. These are the most important messages. I propose a possible agenda that incorporates neurophysiological and behavioral facts and makes adaptive sense, and I propose, in the rule system, an organization the newborn possesses for implementing that agenda.

2 General Method and Procedures

This chapter describes the procedures I used in recording visual activity in the five studies reported. Additionally, the techniques for measuring visual fixation, used in the last three studies, are discussed. All studies were carried out in a laboratory near the newborn nursery in the Cambridge Hospital, Cambridge, Massachusetts, between 1968 and 1972.

The method employed here is based on corneal-reflection photography used orginally by Dodge (1907) and refined through a number of stages, first by Cowey (1963) with monkeys, by Hershenson (1964) who used infrared photography in the Fantz paradigm, by Salapatek and Kessen (1966) to permit measurement of point-of-fixation determinations from filmed records, and finally, by myself (with a great deal of help from some very talented engineers), for infrared television and later point-of-fixation determination from continuous videotape records (Haith, 1969). As an aside I might add that it was not until I could see easily obtained continuous recordings of newborn visual behavior and was impressed with the rapidity and continuity of scanning activity, that I became disillusioned with characterizing this organism as a "static" stimulus *selector* and began to think of the infant more as a "dynamic" information *seeker*.

The reader who is not interested in the details of methodology may wish to turn directly to page 26 where a summary of the methodology is given.

RECORDING OF VISUAL FIXATIONS

General Description. Figure 2.1 displays a schematic outline of the apparatus. The newborn baby lay on his/her back in a padded holder which constrained excessive head movement. The holder was placed on a platform

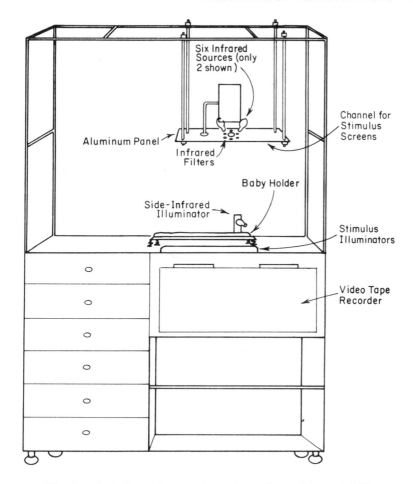

FIG. 2.1.   Illustration of the apparatus used in all five studies reported. The baby lay on the baby holder and viewed the overhead stimulus screens while the (infrared) TV camera recorded the baby's eye onto video tape. The overhead infrared-light sources provided both invisible illumination for recording and reflections on the baby's cornea. These reflections were used for determining the baby's fixation position. The side infrared illuminator enhanced pupil-iris contrast, and the two stimulus illuminators lit the stimulus screen.

inside a special crib. An aluminum plate, 69 cm wide × 61 cm high × .65 cm thick, was mounted horizontally 24 cm above the baby with a threaded 51 cm × 1.25 cm bolt in each corner. The bolts were attached to the 2.54 cm overhead angle-iron framing of the crib. The aluminum plate supported an infrared TV camera, six light sources and filters, and aluminum channels for holding painted window screens. The bottom surface of the aluminum plate was covered with black felt to reduce light reflection and the sides and all metal protrusions were covered with rubber for safety. Light strips (tungsten or fluorescent), covered by plastic diffusers and baffled by black cardboard, were used to illuminate stimuli that were presented overhead. The light strips were mounted just outside, but on the same level, as the central platform of the crib.

TV Camera. The television camera (Shibaden HV-14) was modified to accept an infrared tube (Resistron IND-2000) and was also converted from a random- to a fixed-interlace format. (This latter change was necessary for later transfer of video-tape frames to a videodisc.) The camera was mounted vertically with the center of the lens corresponding to an imaginary vertical line drawn through the center of the stimulus field and the baby's right eye. A 75 mm fl.4 lens (Soligar) was used; it covered a 3.2 cm square field at the plane of the eye which was 25.4 cm away.

A belt-and-gear (PIC belts) arrangement was devised for convenient remote adjustment of the target, beam, and electrical focus knobs on the back of the camera and for the optical focus adjustment on the lens. A 5 cm diameter apperture in the center of the aluminum support panel, below the lens, permitted televising the infant's eye.

Crib, Baby Holder. The crib was 137 cm long × 71 cm wide × 190 cm high and consisted of a bottom wooden cabinet on rubber rollers. The cabinet supported a 91 cm high rectangular frame constructed of 2.5 cm angle iron. This top frame was fitted with 2.5 cm wide metal crossmembers at 46 cm intervals along the side and top. Metal strips were attached to these crossmembers, separated by .65 cm spaces; this arrangement permitted the edge of a .65 cm thick × 46 cm side masonite panel to be slid between the metal bars and then secured by thumbscrews. The availability of the removable panels greatly enhanced flexibility and accessibility to the equipment. The bottom wooden cabinet was fitted with drawers and adjustable shelves and a sliding platform that supported the video-tape recorder. Full-length side panels permitted the cabinet contents to be locked up.

The padded baby holder was placed on a rectangular aluminum panel that was mounted on four Hi-Boy jacks. One jack was mounted under each of the four corners; together, they permitted the flexibility required for height and slant adjustments of the baby's body.

Infrared Lights. Six light sources (Bausch and Lomb Nicholas illuminators) were mounted on the aluminum plate around the camera. These lights served both to illuminate the eye and to mark positions on the stimulus field by reflection from the infant's cornea. Light from 4 of these illuminators passed through 4 apertures in the support panel that occupied the corners of a 10.2 cm vertical × 12.7 cm horizontal (from the baby's position) rectangle around the central camera opening. Two additional apertures were located 19.1 cm to either side of the camera opening. All apertures were 1.9 cm in diameter. Each source light was positioned so that the center of the beam it projected was simultaneously coincident with the predetermined points (the corners of the imaginary rectangle) at the plane of the stimulus screen and the position of the infant's eye, 24.1 cm below the screen. To accomplish the adjustment of each marker beam at the plane of the screen (the most critical adjustment), a grid was placed at screen level and the light positioned until the center of the bulb filament was imaged on the desired point and the circle of light at the plane of the eye was centered in the center of the camera field. An additional light source, added to increase the contrast between the infant's pupil and iris, was placed to the side of the right eye at a distance of from 15-20 cm and as low as possible. Each light beam passed through 2 sets of filters mounted in series 5 Kodak adapter rings. A Corning 7-69 glass filter, which cut off wavelengths beyond 1140 μ (which tend to generate heat), was combined with a custom filter, produced from three layers of Polaroid plastic laminated linear polarizing material (Polaroid filter type HN7); the composite Polaroid filter eliminated wavelengths in the visible region, that is, below 900 mu. With this filter arrangement a "window" of light between 900-1140 mu passed throught the filters; the 6 overhead infrared lights (IR) radiated .17 mcals/sec cm² at the surface of the eye as measured by an Ebbley Instrument Thermopile (#7372). This value is about 1/200 the value of the solar constant, itself judged to be safe.

Stimuli.   The stimulus screen was supported by two aluminum channels each 1.3 cm × 61 cm that were attached to the bottom of the aluminum plate and separated by 50.8 cm. The mounted screen was approximately 1.3 cm in front of the front portion of the camera lens, approximately 24.1 cm above the infant's eye. Stimuli were prepared by spray painting onto window screening that was mounted in an aluminum frame 50.8 cm × 50.8 cm. A flat black enamel and a flat white enamel paint were used. Screens were prepared with masking tape and then sprayed by use of a commercial compressor and spray gun. Care was taken not to apply coats so thickly that the paint ran or clogged up the screen holes. A compromise on thickness of paint was necessitated by consideration of the fact that the thicker the paint the lower the quality of the TV picture (taken through the screen) and the other consideration that the thinner the paint the move visible were the camera lens and infrared beam apertures from the infant's view. Approximately 12-15 coats of paint were sprayed onto each screen.

Video and Audio Recording.   The video output from the TV camera was routed to an Ampex 6000 2.54 cm video-tape recorder and then displayed on a 23 cm Sony TV monitor. The video-recording procedure was standard.

Between stimulus conditions, when the screens were changed, the infant's view of the stimulus field was blocked by a white index card above the eye. Stimulus conditions were indicated on the audio track of the videotape recorder either by the experimenter's voice or by a 60 Hz tone that was generated by an oscillator and connected to the recorder through a switch.

Measuring Eye Position.   A determination of the infant's fixation point at any particular moment required the measurement, from the recorded image of the eye, of the Cartesian-coordinate distance between the center of the pupil and the corneal reflection of at least one of the infrared-marker lights. Figure 2.2 shows a schematic diagram of the sequence of operations between playback of the eye record to final determination and plotting of eye position.

Freezing the TV Image.   A determination of visual fixation was made for each ½ second of real time. In order to obtain the Cartesian-coordinate positions of pupil center and stimulus marker-light reflection it was first

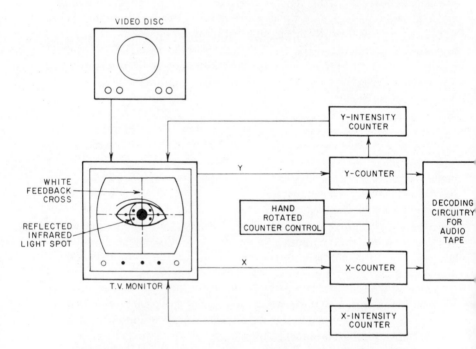

FIG. 2.2.   Illustration of the technique used for measuring fixation location. The videodisc displayed one video frame of the eye. A scorer rotated the counter-control knobs until the vertical and horizontal crosshairs intersected at an infrared reflection or at the center of the pupil. The electronic X- and Y-Counters contained the Cartesian coordinates of the point of intersection. These contents were then recorded onto audio tape for later processing.

necessary to display each TV frame of concern for several seconds. The video-tape record was played back into an MVR videodisc (model VDR-100S-2A) that was set to sample 1 out of every 15 frames (that is, 2 successive video fields approximately each ½ second). The disc could store up to 500 video frames.

Measurement of Cartesian-Coordinate Position of Light Reflections and Pupil Center. With a single TV frame displayed on the TV screen (Conrac 48 cm video monitor), the scorer proceeded to make the measurements of concern with electromechanical aids. Before beginning to measure fixation positions for a subject, the scorer measured the position of all 6 infrared reflections on each of 10 frames. These measurements provided scale factors for later computer calculation of the ratio of the number of machine units to the number of cm in the stimulus field. The scorer then proceeded to measure the position of the center of the pupil and the infrared reflection closest to the center of the pupil on every frame; this choice of closest light as reference point for each frame was made on the basis of prior adult-calibration data which showed it to yield the greatest precision of measurement.

The scoring of a particular point is described first in general and then in more technical terms. Superimposed on the displayed TV picture of the eye was a pair of thin, white vertical and horizontal crosshairs. The scorer could adjust the position of these crosshairs by rotating two knobs that were mounted in a small box. As a knob was rotated, it moved a crosshair and changed the contents of a binary counter that indicated the vertical or horizontal position of the line. Measurement of a point, then, was accomplished by adjusting the crosshairs until they intersected at the point of interest. The contents of the binary counters were then stored by pressing a button which recorded their settings as pulse trains (Lentz & Haith, 1969) on an audio-tape recorder. This scheme produced 525 points on the Y axis and 625 points on the X axis. One machine unit was roughly equivalent to .63 cm in the infant's visual field. Decoding, editing, calculation, plotting, and statistical analyses were carried out by further processing with the aid of PDP9 and IBM 360/70 computers. This description applies to scoring of a "perfect" eye. In actuality, various problems were encountered in making judgments for scoring purposes. A discussion of these problems is included in the following section.

A logic-flow diagram of the measurement circuitry is shown in Fig. 2.3. The scoring of a point is initiated when the scorer presses the X- or Y-Seek Button on the control box; each button simultaneously enables the related Y-Seek Counter or X-Seek Counter, to accept inputs.

Consider only the Y-axis measurement. The circuitry alternates between a display and a seek mode on alternate video frames. When the Y-Seek Button is depressed, the Y-Seek Counter "finds" the setting of the Y-time potentiometer on every other frame as follows. The Vertical Synch pulse goes

VERT. SEEK DISPLAY TIMING

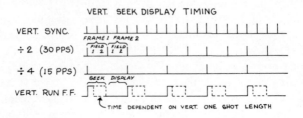

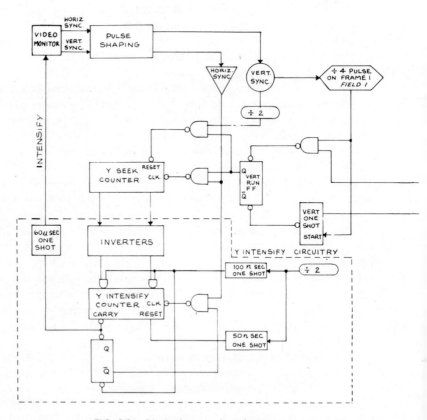

FIG. 2.3.   Block diagram of scoring apparatus.

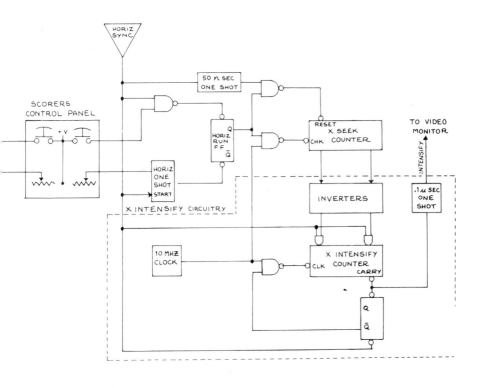

HORIZ
SYNC

50 n SEC
ONE SHOT

SCORERS
CONTROL PANEL

+V

HORIZ
RUN
F F
Q
Q̄

RESET
X SEEK
COUNTER
CHK

TO VIDEO
MONITOR

INTENSIFY

HORIZ
ONE
SHOT
START

X INTENSIFY CIRCUITRY

INVERTERS

.1μ SEC
ONE
SHOT

10 MHZ
CLOCK

X INTENSIFY
COUNTER
CLK
CARRY

Q
Q̄

21

through a divide-by-four circuit, which generates a pulse coincident with the beginning of field one on every other frame. This pulse starts a One-Shot that, in turn, resets and enables the Y-Seek Counter. With the Y-Seek Counter enabled, the Horizontal Synch pulses increment the Y-Seek Counter once for each horizontal line (15,750 times/second) until the Y One-Shot times out. The duration of the One-Shot is a function of the setting of the adjustable Y-time knob on the scorer's control box. Hence, with the Y-Seek Button depressed, the Y-Seek Counter resets to "0" at the beginning of every other frame (field 1 of, for example, frames 1, 3, 5, 7, etc.) and is incremented by one with each successive horizontal line until the vertical One-Shot, controlled by the scorer, times out. The Seek Counter now contains the number of lines from the top of the screen to the line on the screen corresponding to the position of the flying spot when the One-Shot timed out.

On intervening, display, frames (frames 2, 4, 6, 8, etc.) the Y-Feedback Circuitry generates a white horizontal line on the TV monitor to indicate the current setting of the Y-Seek Counter as follows. The 12 bits of the Y-Intensity Counter are connected to the 12 bits of the Y-Seek Counter through inverters. The Vertical Synch pulses pass through a divide-by-two circuit that generates an output pulse coincident with the beginning of field one of every frame. This pulse enables the Y-Intensity Counter to accept the shifted complement of the Y-Seek Counter. The Y-Intensity Counter then counts Horizontal Synch pulses until it reaches "0" (the same number of counts contained in the Y-Seek Counter). When "0" is reached, a carry pulse is generated that, through the 60 μsec One-Shot and the Video Amplifier, presents a 1.5 volt signal to the gun of the cathode-ray tube (CRT) in the Video Monitor for the duration of one horizontal line. The carry pulse also disables gate one and the Y-Intensity Counter so that additional Horizontal Synch pulses are not counted until the next relevant Vertical Synch pulse occurs. The contents of the Seek Counter can only be changed when the Y-Seek Button is depressed; however, the Intensity Counter runs continuously, thereby always generating a white line at the current setting of the Seek Counter.

With a few exceptions, the vertical line is positioned and displayed in a similar manner. The Horizontal Synch pulse provides similar functions to that provided by the Vertical Synch pulse for the Y Counter. That is, with the X-Seek Button depressed, a Horizontal Synch pulse starts the X One-Shot, resets the X-Seek Counter to "0," and enables the X-Seek Counter to accept pulses from a 10 MHZ clock. The X-Seek Counter increments with each clock pulse until the Horizontal One-Shot times out. Since the flying CRT spot requires 62.5 μsec to produce each horizontal line, approximately 625 points can be measured along the X axis. The operation of the X-Intensity Counter is similar to that of the Y-Intensity Counter. However, one difference is that the

X-carry pulse activates a One-Shot for approximately 0.1 μsec to produce a thin white dot on every horizontal line at the current X-counter setting.

When the scorer has adjusted the white crosshairs so that they intersect at the point of interest, a record button is pressed and the contents of the Y-Seek Counter and the X-Seek Counter are recorded onto audio tape in a pulse code (Lentz & Haith, 1969).The content of a third, 10-bit counting register, is also stored. The first bit of this counter indicates whether the contents of the counter represent a special code (previous frame a mistake, subject number, condition, etc.) or a real measurement. When a code is being recorded, the code numbers are set into the counter by toggle switches. If a measurement is being recorded, three bits of this counter are set by toggle switches to indicate which infrared light (reference light) is scored on the current frame. The remaining six bits indicate the number of the current frame. After recording the coordinates for a particular frame, a button is pressed which advances the disk to the next TV frame and increments the frame counter by one.

Calibration of this procedure with adults revealed a level of precision comparable to that reported by Salapatek, Haith, Maurer, and Kessen (1972), using film procedures and a Vanguard Motion Analyzer for data reduction. As previously known (Salapatek et al., 1972; Slater & Findlay, 1972), there was a slight but variable bias to the right of the point actually fixated when the right eye was measured. (All studies reported here measured fixation of the right eye.) The scoring procedure required approximately 15-20 seconds/frame. Including time to transfer the original record from the video tape to the videodisc, adjust equipment, make scale-factor measurements, score 540 frames (studies 3, 4, and 5 required 270 seconds of good recording), make corrections, take breaks, etc., approximately 4½ hours were required to measure each subject's record. An additional ½ hour was required to transfer the audiotape recording to a PDP9 computer and approximately 1 hour more was needed to find and correct errors. The coordinate of each fixation point was calculated by the PDP9 computer and then these data were dataphoned to an IBM 360/370 computer that was programmed to graph the fixation points with a dataplotter and to carry out data analyses.

Problems in Scoring the Eye Records.   Since the reflection of the infrared lights comprised relatively discrete points, few problems were encountered in measuring the positions of the IR reflections. Exceptions occurred rarely when the camera was out of focus. If the lights formed a blur, it was assumed that the eye or head was moving at that moment, and the frame was not scored.

The determination of pupil center was more of a problem. Pupil-iris contrast was sometimes marginal making it difficult to determine where the edge of the pupil lay. When marginal images were obtained, a 23-cm TV monitor was used in addition to the 48-cm scoring monitor. The smaller monitor tended to sharpen contrast, thereby aiding the scorer in viewing the larger monitor. Additionally, parts of the pupil were sometimes obscured by the upper or lower lid, making judgment more difficult.

Careful adjustment of the infant's head during recording attenuated the problem of lid obstruction. The tilt of the baby's head was adjusted so that when the infant's eye was near the center of his/her visual field (as indicated in the TV picture of the eye), the reflections of the IR lights were centered approximately in the eye socket.[1] Frequently, we found it more convenient to place a diaper under the infant's head for forward tilt, or under the baby's shoulders for backward tilt, than to work with the Hi-Boy jacks.

An additional problem in scoring was that, as the eye fixated away from visual center, the pupil appeared increasingly ellipsoid rather than round. When the pupil appeared to be round (that is, when the subject was looking near the center of the field), a scorer judged pupil center by simply bisecting the pupil on the vertical and horizontal axes with the vertical and horizontal crosshairs. When the pupil was distorted, the scorer used a combination of criteria to place a crosshair. The quadrant of the eye closest to the center of the camera field was given greatest emphasis for a judgment, other portions tending to appear more extended than normal. If possible, the scorer attempted to combine this criterion with the greatest extent of black, top and bottom or left and right, for a placement. When greatest extent at the top and bottom did not correspond, the crosshair was placed between them.

Each scorer underwent a training regimen prior to scoring experimental data. A calibration tape of an adult eye was first prepared in which the eye was recorded as it looked at predetermined locations. A scorer then scored these points, plotted them, and determined the error based on the distance from the plotted point to the known fixation point. The scorer then went back to the original calibration tape and reset the crosshairs for each fixation point, both at where they had previously been placed, and then, where the scorer knew they should be placed for errorless measurement. By this procedure, the

---

[1]Pacifier sucking helped to stabilize the position of the head. Non-nutritive sucking was measured through a closed-pressure tube-and-nipple arrangement that was connected to a Statham P23AC pressure transducer. The transducer output was recorded by a Grass Model 7 DC Preamplifier and Driver Amplifier onto chart paper. Simultaneously, the voltage changes appearing at the polygraph pen were recorded onto audio tape (Tandberg, 64X) through a Vetter Model 3 FM converter which permitted later chart-recording at different speeds. The audio and video records were synchronized by a "start" signal recorded on the audio channel of the video-tape recorder and on one channel of the audio-tape recorder. The sucking data and their relation to newborn scanning have been published elsewhere (Mendelson & Haith, 1975). Temperature in the experimental room varied from 70°-75°F. Ambient sound level, measured at the position of the infant's head, varied between 56-58 db.

scorer could learn what criteria could best be used for most accurate placement and what criteria had previously been used that produced error. The final stage was for the scorer to repeat scoring of the tape. This procedure was repeated until error in measurement had become quite small.

The problem of error in this procedure has been discussed at length by Slater and Findlay (1972) and by Salapatek et al. (1972). A brief discussion is included here. First of all, it is known that the assumption of this procedure— that a line drawn backward through the center of the pupil and lens to the retina will strike the fovea—is, on the average, incorrect. In the adult, the fovea, on the average, lies about 4.5° to the temporal side of the optic center of the retina and about 1.5° below it.

Using our procedure, with the right eye, the calculated points of fixation could be expected to be placed somewhat to the right and below the actual point of fixation. For the infant, it has been argued that the embryological fact that the fovea shifts toward optical center from an even more distant position may make matters even worse (Slater & Findlay, 1972). However, the developmental data on anatomical changes after birth are quite dated and are based on very few infants. Additionally, the data were obtained on babies who died of unknown reasons, which leaves the possibility open that their development up to the time of death was not normal.

A second problem arises from the fact that the infrared lights are reflected from a spherical plane formed by the cornea such that the image of the infrared lights appears behind the pupillary opening. Thus, there is a parallax problem as the eye moves away from the central visual axis. As the eye moves to the temporal side, it increasingly appears as though it is even further displaced from center than it really is, thus adding to the error produced by inconvenient anatomy. The two types of error begin to cancel when the eye is oriented toward visual center and reverse as it moves further to the nasal side.

If the problems introduced by these errors were standard, then we could, as has been suggested (Slater & Findlay, 1972), make straightforward corrections on our data. However, there is subject variability in the anatomical relations at the retina, in the pupil-corneal distances, in corneal curvature, imperfections in the cornea, and so on. Moreover, people differ in what portions of the foveal and parafoveal regions are used for fixation. Salapatek et al. (1972) ran literally thousands of calibrations with adults in which subjects were asked to fixate known points in the visual field and then the technique just described was used to measure their fixation positions. When the error in calculated position against known position was plotted, it was different for different subjects and sometimes in opposite directions than expected from the anatomical and optical considerations I have presented. Thus, error corrections based on averaged data may be valid for correcting a group statistic, but there are serious problems in using such corrections on individual subject data. Given the limits of our knowledge concerning newborn ocular and retinal anatomy and the fact that precise calibration data could not be obtained, I felt it best to use the raw data rather than to use corrections based on unvalidated assumptions.

Summary of Eye Recording and Measurement Methodology. A summary is given here of the physical setup, the recording procedure, and the technique for measuring eye position. The infant was placed in a specially equipped crib that contained facilities for stimulus presentation and for overhead mounting of an infrared TV camera and infrared lights (see Fig. 2.1). As the infant scanned a stimulus that had been spray painted onto window screening, the TV camera recorded the image of the infant's right eye from behind the screen. Infrared lights, mounted around the camera, provided invisible light for recording the eye. Additionally, the reflection of these lights on the cornea provided positional reference points of the baby's visual field. These reflections could later be used to determine the baby's fixation point on the infant's visual field.

After observation, the video-taped record of the baby's eye was transferred to a videodisc. The videodisc sampled the video tape twice each second. Then, each sample was displayed on a TV monitor, and a scorer measured the Cartesian coordinates of the center of the pupil and of the closest infrared-light reflection. These measurements were made by rotating knobs that positioned white vertical and horizontal crosshairs on the TV screen (see Fig. 2.2). The coordinates were stored electronically on audio tape and then transferred to a computer. Computer programs calculated the infant's fixation location on each frame and re-created the scanning sequence by plotting the fixations on paper over a drawing of the original stimulus.

3

Study 1,
How Newborns Scan in Darkness:
Newborn Scanning in Darkness
and on Formless Light Fields

This is the first of five studies described, as mentioned in Chapter 1. My general strategy in all of this research was to use farily simple visual situations so as to maximize the likelihood of finding natural regularities in the organization of behavior. Given that I consider stimuli to constrain visual activity, it made sense to begin with the simplest situations possible and then to introduce increasingly more complex situations. In Study 1, I was interested in learning about the newborn's visual activity in the absence of light or visual form. The absence of light is clearly the most uncomplicated "visual" condition of all with homogeneous, or unstructured, light the next step up. Some data exist on newborn visual activity in homogeneous light; these come from studies that have used formless stimulus fields for control comparison with experimental periods in which geometric forms were presented (Kessen et al., 1972; Salapatek, 1968; Salapatek & Kessen, 1966). Newborns scan homogeneous fields extensively, primarily along the horizontal axis, moving their eyes at least once each second; thus, we know that the presence of contour is not necessary for visual activity.

When the present study was undertaken, there had been no examination of what infants do in the absence of light (and, obviously form), that is, in total darkness. How newborns behave visually in darkness is of theoretical interest in understanding the mechanisms controlling eye movements and the degree to which visual scanning is controlled by internal as opposed to external determinants. Few maintain any longer that newborns can not see, but it has been widely held that the newborn is a reflex organism, visually, and that scanning activity reflects tropisms toward light. By this argument, scanning in homogeneous fields might reflect the newborn's tendency to try to find the brightest portion of the field, in this case, an endless search. But that same argument, taken literally, would predict that the newborn should be visually inactive in darkness.

Perceptual theorists have not concerned themselves with visual behavior in darkness for obvious reasons. Hebb (1949) held that visual perception begins when a figure/ground relation is detected. Piaget (1951) and most reasonable people agree that "knowledge" of objects, apart from their immediate perceptibility, is not possible at birth. By these theorists, then, one might also expect visual inactivity or, perhaps, even a tendency for newborns to close their eyes in darkness. Others (Jeffrey, 1968; Kessen, 1966) have suggested that newborn's eye movements may be produced by peripheral visual stimulation when the response to a presently fixated segment of the visual field habituates. By this argument, even if the baby's eyes were to remain open in dark, one might expect them to remain stationary because peripheral visual stimuli would be eliminated.

Some years ago, I (Haith, 1973) presented preliminary evidence that, in fact, newborns as young as 8 hours of age open their eyes in darkness and move them actively and frequently. I argued that the newborn might be programmed at birth to search for light in a dark situation if awake and alert. The implication is that the newborn comes fully equipped to engage in active visual search even when stimuli are not available to "determine" visual activity. However, these observations were made on only a few babies and stray light was not rigorously controlled. The present study was carried out to examine more formally a substantial number of subjects under carefully controlled light and dark conditions.

METHOD

Subjects. The subjects were 16 full-term awake and apparently normal human infants, between 24 and 96 hours of age, born at the Cambridge Hospital, Cambridge, Massachusetts. Fifteen additional infants were observed but their data were not used because they cried ($n = 2$), did not meet the criterion for wakefulness (20 seconds of open eyes during the experiment, $n = 5$), or because the equipment failed or picture quality was not adequate ($n = 8$).

Apparatus and Stimuli. The stimuli were 50.8 cm × 50.8 cm screens prepared by spray painting. Two screens were used, one black and one white. The two screen brightnesses were used to determine to what extent intensity values alone could account for differences found between light-on and light-off conditions. Great care was exercised to remove all sources of visible light that were not used for illuminating the stimulus screens. The room was carefully light-proofed as were the boxes containing the infrared illuminators. All pilot lamps were removed from equipment. The TV monitor was turned off during dark periods.

A potentiometer was used to turn the tungsten stimulus lamps (60W, 45.72 cm covered by .08 cm plastic diffusing material) on and off at a gradual rate. A 110 voltage source for the lamps was routed through a variable transformer that reduced the maximum voltage to about 100 volts. This voltage was chosen because, at that level, a gradual rotation of the potentiometer seemed to produce a smooth light/dark transition through the full range of illumination used. The rheostat was limited to supply 60 volts to the stimulus lamps at full onset. Photometric readings, taken by a Honeywell Photometer on the black and white screens were .24 cd/m² and 3.08 cd/m², respectively.

To an adult, lying in the position of the newborn with lights off, nothing on the stimulus field was visible after 2 minutes of dark adaptation (the duration used in the study). A switch, controlled by an experimenter, energized an event pen on a polygraph to indicate the initiation of light onset and offset conditions. Other specifics of the eye-recording apparatus and procedure are described in Chapter 2.

Procedure.   A newborn baby was selected from the nursery among those who were awake and whose mothers had signed releases permitting their babies' participation in the study. The baby was freshly diapered, if necessary, and then the baby's basinet was rolled to the observation room. Babies were observed from 15 minutes to 1 1/2 hours prior to feeding and almost always before the 2:00 PM meal.

Because the position of the infant's eye could not be watched on the TV monitor during dark periods, it was necessary to exercise fairly strict control of head movement. It was also necessary to control hand movements so the hands could not cover the eye. Therefore, the baby was placed in a circumstraint circumcision board; a concave padded support was added for the baby's head. Stability in the position of the baby's head was also facilitated by a nipple, held at midline, by an experimenter. The baby's arms were restrained near his/her sides by broad rubber bands covered with Velcro. The infant's left eye was covered by a Telfa gauze pad.

The baby was positioned under the stimulus apparatus so that the right eye was centered in the visual field of the TV camera. Frequently, it was necessary to adjust the Hi-Boy jacks that supported the aluminum plate and the circumcision board, or to place a diaper(s) under the newborn's shoulders. Adjustments were made so that the baby's eye was parallel to the plane of the stimulus as indicated by a centered reflection of the infrared lights on the TV image of the eye. The infrared side light was adjusted to optimize picture quality. After the polygraph, video tape, and audio tape recorders were started, the experiment began.

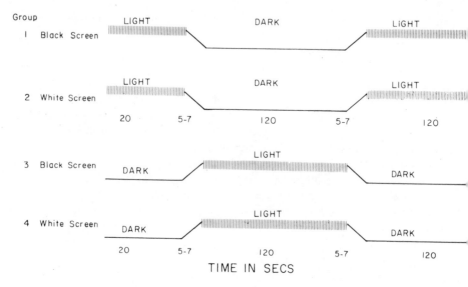

FIG. 3.1.   Timing chart for the experimental conditions in Study 1. Groups 1 and 3 were presented a black screen and groups 2 and 4 were presented a white screen.

The experimental sequence and the stimuli that were presented during light periods were determined by which of the four groups the infant had been randomly assigned to. Infants in groups 1 and 3 were presented the black screen during light-on periods, and infants in groups 2 and 4 were presented the white screen.

Figure 3.1 shows a timing chart of the experimental conditions. Groups 1 and 2 received a light-on condition for 20 seconds followed by total darkness for 120 seconds and then light for 120 seconds. Groups 3 and 4 received light-off for 20 seconds followed by light for 120 seconds and then darkness for 120 seconds. The transitions from light to dark and dark to light were gradual and continuous, occurring over an interval of 5-7 seconds. After the experiment, a Polaroid picture was taken of the baby. The picture and a Harvard "diploma" for the baby were offered to the mother as tokens of appreciation for her cooperation.

RESULTS

The effect of the experimental manipulations on four dependent variables was examined. These were (1) degree of eye opening, (2) degree of eye control, (3) sharpness of eye movements, and (4) size of eye movement. An observer viewed the video-tape records and made independent judgments of these four

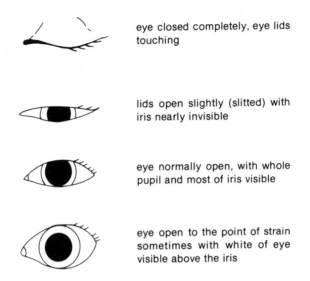

eye closed completely, eye lids touching

lids open slightly (slitted) with iris nearly invisible

eye normally open, with whole pupil and most of iris visible

eye open to the point of strain sometimes with white of eye visible above the iris

FIG. 3.2.   Categories of eye opening.

variables on separate occasions at a real-time rate of about one judgment each 2.5 seconds, as signalled by a metronome. A total of 45 judgments were made for each 120-second period. Analyses on these four variables revealed that newborns opened their eyes more in darkness than in light and moved them actively. In darkness, eye movements were more controlled, sharper, and somewhat smaller than in light. Whereas visual behavior in light was different from that in the dark, the relative brightness of the visual field in light had virtually no effect. More details on the effect of the experimental manipulations are now discussed.

Degree of Eye Opening.[1]   The degree of eye opening was judged on a scale from 1 to 4 as follows: 1 = eye closed completely, eye lids touching; 2 = lids open slightly (slitted) with iris nearly invisible; 3 = eye normally open, with whole pupil and most of iris visible; 4 = eye open to the point of strain sometimes with white of eye visible about the iris. Figure 3.2 shows the degree of eye opening assigned to each category.

One of the most interesting findings was that 56% of the observations during dark were assigned to category 4—eye opening to the point of strain—

[1]The reliability data calculated on this measure and the other measures used in this experiment were lost when I moved my laboratories from Harvard University to the University of Denver. Agreement scores between two observers scoring the same data at the same time were in excess of 90% for all four variables. More detailed reliability on these same measures with newborns for a similar paradigm are reported in the results section of Study 2.

TABLE 3.1
Percentage of Judgments in Each of Four
Degrees of Eye-Open Categories for
the Dark and Light Conditions in Study 1

Light Condition	Category			
	1	2	3	4
Light	19%	22%	41%	17%
Dark	4%	11%	30%	56%

whereas only 17% of the observations during light fell in this category. Table 3.1 gives the average percentage for each category of degree of eye opening for the light and dark condition, respectively.

In order to examine the time course of degree of eye opening, 6 time-block totals were calculated by adding together 7 degree-of-opening scores; thus each block represented approximately 17.5 seconds. The block scores formed the basic datum for a mixed 2 X 2 X 2 X 6 analysis of variance with Screen Intensity and Sequence of Presentation as between-subject variables and Lighting Condition and Time Blocks as within-subject variables.

The analysis of variance revealed a significant Lighting effect, $F(1,12) = 29.1$, $p < .001$), a significant Block effect, $F(5,60) = 7.8$, $p < .01$, and a significant Sequence X Lighting interaction, $F(1,12) = 11.3$, $p < .01$. Subjects opened their eyes more widely during darkness than in light and there was a tendency for eyes to be open wider during the early time blocks of a light condition. A graph of degree of opening as a function of screen brightness, light condition, and time is shown in Fig. 3.3.

The means forming the Sequence X Lighting interaction are shown in Table 3.2. It can be seen that the difference between light and dark conditions was greater when the dark condition appeared first, but the direction of the relation between eye opening and light and dark was the same for both sequence conditions.

Importantly, neither the screen Brightness factor, $F(1,12) = 0.00$, nor the Brightness X Light condition interaction, $F(1,12) = .64$, was stable. (In fact, the scores were almost identical.) Unexpectedly, in the light-on condition, eye opening was slightly less for the black screen than for the white screen, perhaps reflecting original baseline differences (as seen at left of Fig. 3.3). The point is that striking differences in ambient illumination between the black- and white-screen groups produced no difference in the light-on condition. This finding suggests that the difference in eye opening between the dark and light conditions was not produced by a simple function relating brightness and eye opening; rather, it seems that a qualitative as opposed to a quantitative difference between light and dark was reflected in this measure.

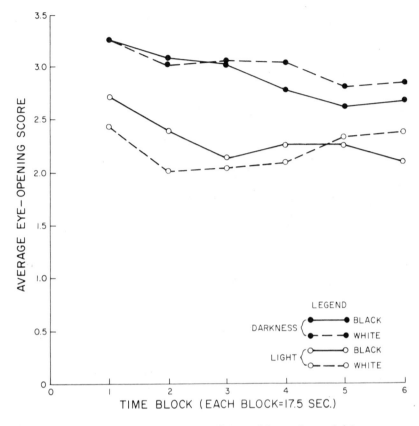

FIG. 3.3. The effect of the dark and the light conditions and screen brightness on eye opening over time in Study 1.

Eye Control.   Judgments of eye control were made by assigning a number to each 2.5-second time segment that indicated whether the eyes were closed, open and in control, or open and out of control. The "out-of-control" assignment was made if, during any portion of the 2.5-second period, 2 or more eye jerks occurred at either the temporal or nasal side of the eye. Out-of-

TABLE 3.2
Average Subgroub Eye-Open Score for the Dark and
Light Conditions and the Sequences for Study 1

| | Light Condition | |
Sequence	Light	Dark
Light/Dark	20.79	22.83
Dark/Light	15.29	24.06

TABLE 3.3

Percentage of Eye Movements in Each of the Degree-of-Control Categories for the Dark and Light Conditions and for the White and Black Screens for Study 1

	Light Condition					
	Light			Dark		
Screen Brightness	Eye Closed	In-Control	Out-of Control	Eye Closed	In-Control	Out-of Control
White	18%	56%	26%	7%	92%	1%
Black	11%	70%	19%	8%	91%	1%

control movements consisted of nystagmic-jerk sequences, which typically occurred on the temporal side but occasionally on the nasal side. An analysis was made of in-control vs. out-of-control eye movements. For this analysis, segments were excluded in which no movement occurred.

Table 3.3 displays the mean percentage of in-control and out-of-control eye movements and the percentage of time the eyes were closed as a function of Screen Brightness and Lighting conditions. Four babies had fewer than 10 movements that could be judged during the light-on conditions because their eyes were closed the remaining time. These babies were evenly distributed among the two Screen-Brightness groups. Their data from neither the dark nor the light periods were used for this analysis.

The results were quite clear: nystagmic sequences occurred 23% of the time during light periods, but less than 1% of the time during dark periods. All babies displayed a higher percentage of out-of-control movements during light periods than during dark periods. Although a greater percentage of in-control movements occurred in light when the black screen was present, there was a great deal of overlap between groups and the difference was not stable..

Type of Eye Movement.   Judgments of type of eye movement were made for those segments in which the eyes were open, moved, and in control by assignment to three categories: (1) jerky movement: the eye moves sharply with both the initiation and termination having an abrupt quality; (2) smooth movement: the eye movement has a definite initiation and termination, associated with normal saccades, but seems more controlled than (1) and is not jerky or abrupt; (3) slow drift: the eye movement has a somewhat indefinite initiation and termination, is slower than (1) and (2), and often, unlike (1) or (2), has a strong vertical component.

Table 3.4 displays the mean percentage of each type of movement as a function of the Intensity and Lighting conditions. Each mean was based on six babies' scores. The "no movement" score is a percentage of all eligible

TABLE 3.4

Percentage of Judgments in Four Categories of Eye Movement for the Dark and Light Conditions and for the White and Black screens for Study 1

| | Light Condition | | | | | | | |
| | Light | | | | Dark | | | |
Screen Brightness	No Movement	Jerky	Smooth	Drift	No Movement	Jerky	Smooth	Drift
White	19%	72%	8%	19%	19%	50%	30%	20%
Black	18%	68%	12%	20%	26%	30%	27%	42%

segments. Other percentages are presented in terms of total number of segments in which the eye moved.

There was a clear tendency for babies to make more smooth and fewer jerky movements in the dark than in the light. All 12 babies had a smaller percentage of jerky movements during dark than light periods (mean of 40% and 70%, respectively), and all 12 babies had a larger percentage of smooth movements during dark periods (mean of 28.5% and 10%, respectively). Finally, although there was a somewhat higher percentage of slow drift movements in darkness than in light (mean of 30% and 19.5%, respectively), there was a good deal of overlap between groups.

Screen brightness made little apparent difference; in fact, the percentage of each type of movement for the black- and white-screen groups was surprisingly consistent between the groups for such a small n. The larger difference between these groups when lights were off seems principally attributable to one baby in the white-screen group who contributed a score of 87% jerky movements and 5% drift movements to his subgroup average.

Size of Eye Movement.   For each 2.5-second time segment, a decision was made about whether the eye had made a small movement or a large movement or had remained stationary. A large movement was one in which the initiation-to-termination distance was greater than 1/4 of the diameter of the iris. Nystagmic eye movement periods were not used in this analysis. The mean percentage of eye movement falling into each category as a function of the Intensity and Lighting conditions is shown in Table 3.5.

A 2 X 2 mixed analysis of variance was carried out on the percentage of large movement scores, with Light Condition and Screen Brightness as the major factors. Although the absolute difference between light-conditions was not great, a higher percentage of large movements did occur in light than in dark (32% vs. 21%, respectively, $F(1,10) = 8.4$, $p < .05$).

TABLE 3.5
Percentage of Judgment in Three Size-of-Movement Categories for the Dark and Light Conditions and for the White and Black Screens for Study 1

	Light Condition					
	Light			Dark		
Screen Brightness	No Movement	Small Movement	Large Movement	No Movement	Small Movement	Large Movement
White	19%	45%	36%	19%	56%	24%
Black	18%	54%	28%	25%	57%	18%

DISCUSSION

The findings of the present study clearly supported my preliminary observations reported in 1968 (Haith, 1973). When newborn infants are placed in a totally dark situation, they open their eyes widely and move them actively, typically with saccades that are separated by firm fixations. The differential effect of light and dark on the degree of eye opening was clear and consistent. Unexpectedly, a high proportion of judgments in dark (56%) were in the "eye open to the point of strain" category as compared to a much lower proportion in light (17%). This difference cannot simply be attributed to light level, because a strong difference in Screen Brightness had only a slight effect on the percentage of category 4 assignments (23% vs. 11% for black and white screens, respectively, during light-on periods) and virtually no effect on the summary eye-opening measure. Within limits, whether light is present or absent may be more important than the brightness of that light.

Exactly why the newborns engaged in "strained" opening of the eyes in darkness is not clear. It seems unlikely that detection of dim stimuli would be facilitated by eye widening (although the pupillary opening was partially obscured for categories 1 and 2); perhaps the strained opening reflects a general-system orienting or tenseness in an alert baby who is receiving no visual input. Other data also support the idea that the contrast between light and dark represents a categorical difference rather than simply a difference between two levels on the same quantitative dimension. The eye-control data were exceptionally consistent, revealing a much higher percentage of out-of-control eye movement in a formless light field than in darkness (22.5% vs. 1%), but no effect of Screen Brightness. Since there was nothing to look at in either the light or dark conditions, this finding is intriguing.

Although I treat this matter in more depth later, let me suggest here the possibility that eye control in darkness may reflect the operation of neural organization that is not dependent on external input for coordinated looking.[2] However, in light, control of looking activity may be "given over" to a mechanism that is governed by external stimuli. By this line of reasoning, the lit formless visual field "turned on" the stimulus-dependent looking system but did not provide the external input required to control that system.

The findings with the eye-control measure require qualification of the frequent statement that the newborn's visual behavior is uncontrolled. The data support this notion only when the newborn is in formless light or perhaps

---

[2]Roffwarg, Muzio, and Dement (1966) have proposed a similar internally driven mechanism to account for the high level of REM sleep in newborns, which presumably reflects organized neural firing in the absence of external stimulation. The higher incidence of REM sleep in younger infants is presumably adaptive inasmuch as mature neural pathways must be primed to be maintained, and sufficient external input is not available at birth.

when there is no salient object for the baby to fixate on (or the object is outside the range of fixation capability; Haynes, White, & Held, 1965). However, it is clear from this study that controlled scanning in darkness is typical and our later studies show that controlled scanning is also typical in light when an adequate stimulus is available.[3]

The movement-sharpness measure also indicated poor eye control by newborns in light even when nystagmic movements were not considered. All infants produced a greater number of jerky, abrupt, "darting" eye movements in light than in dark. Conversely, movements in dark were smoother and, seemingly, more under control. Again, screen brightness made little difference. The percentage of "no-movement" judgments under light and dark conditions was quite similar, supporting my earlier observation that infants actively move their eyes in total darkness. A comment concerning my observation scale may avoid some confusion. Since time segments were 2.5 seconds long, and approximately 20% of the judgments were of the "no-movement" variety, one might challenge the statement that I and others have made regarding the higher frequency with which infants make eye movements every 1/2 second. That statement is based on precise eye-movement measures or electrophysiological techniques. The measure used in this study was not as precise, and very slight eye movements were probably missed; perhaps this category of eye movement should be considered to represent both zero and very small eye movements.

This brings us to the final variable of interest: size of eye movement. Although this variable revealed smaller absolute differences in percentages between light and dark groups, there was a stable difference, with a higher percentage of large movements occurring during light periods.

These four variables are not, of course, completely independent of one another. Yet, they are not totally dependent either. Together, they give us a picture of the newborn baby as an organism who displays very active, perhaps intense, controlled scanning of the "visual field" in darkness. Perhaps two of the newborn's most elementary rules or instructions are: (1) "if awake and alert and light not too bright, open eyes," and (2) "if in darkness, search." One might ask what the infant is searching for. Without assuming that the baby "knows," I argued initially that the baby might be searching for light (Haith, 1973). However, given the data on eye opening that suggest such intensity of "purpose" (eyes open to the point of strain), and the relatively small eye movements, it may be that the baby is wired to search in a fashion that optimizes the likelihood of finding subtle stimuli, such as shadows in

---

[3]One note of caution: the 22% out-of-control figure in light indicates the number of 2.5-second time segments in which nystagmus was judged to have occurred. This does not necessarily mean that nystagmus occurred 22% of the total time. However, at least two out-of-control movements were required for this judgment, and such eye movements usually appeared in groups of several.

darkness. If the newborn were attempting to find "light," per se, one would not expect the kind of detailed looking that I found here; rather, large sweeps and even a minimal use of peripheral vision would seem sufficient.

In contrast to the appearance of the newborn in darkness, the newborn in a formless light field can be characterized as an organism whose eyes are often either out of control or engaged in abrupt darting movements around the visual field. These movements are larger than in darkness, and the infant seems to be less intense. Perhaps, the "rule" for an infant in formless light is to "search for contours," primitive form, for which larger sweeping and fast-darting movements seem appropriate.

To the best of my knowledge, no substantial neurophysiological data exist to support the argument that different neural mechanisms control eye movements in light and darkness. But there are suggestive data. Single-cell recording in area 17 of awake monkeys has revealed some cells that fire during rapid eye movements in light but not in darkness (Wurtz, 1968). (Chapter 9 contains a more extensive discussion concerning Area 17.) Noda, Freeman, and Creutzfeldt (1972), recording in single cells of the visual cortex in cats, found a small percentage of units (10%) that fired only with rapid eye movements; they did not respond to gratings of any orientation, to relatively high velocity movement of gratings, or to shadows. These cells were activated most dramatically when a checkerboard stimulus was in the field, but some also fired during absolute darkness, although with a longer latency following eye movement and in a less time-locked fashion than when the stimulus was present. The interesting fact is that about half of these cells did not fire in darkness. Unfortunately, the dark condition was used as a control to establish that some cells would fire in the absence of visual pattern, rather than to compare neural activity in unpatterned light and darkness. However, the finding that saccade-related cells fire differentially in patterned light and darkness lends some credence to the notion that different movement-related neural systems may be operative in light and in dark.

Independent of whether these neurophysiological findings are relevant, the behavioral facts seem clear. Babies are wired at birth to open their eyes, even in darkness, and to move them over the "visual field" in a controlled fashion. Such activity probably optimizes the detection of subtle stimuli. Whatever the case, the baby engages in activity that optimizes the likelihood of the baby's detecting stimuli if they exist; the baby's visual activity does not hinge on the presentation of a stimulus for energization. When light is available, but contours are not, eye movements become somewhat disorganized and uncontrolled. The strong differential effects of light and dark, considered with the null effect of a log-unit difference in Brightness between the light and dark fields, suggest that light and dark are *qualitatively* different conditions for the newborn, not two levels along a simple quantitative dimension of Brightness.

4

Study 2, How Newborns Respond to Rate of Visual Change: Newborn Response to Rapid Onset and Offset of Light and State of Alertness

The findings from Study 1 suggested three relatively basic rules for visual activity that the baby obeys at birth: (1) if awake and alert, open eyes; (2) if no light, search (the coordination of eye movements being determined by an internal search mechanism); (3) if there is light, search for edges.

Study 1 employed the most elementary visual stimulus conditions I could imagine, but possibly not the most elementary biological condition. That is, only alert babies were observed, as implied by rule 1 above. However, it seemed possible that a more general rule might apply; that is, a baby in any state might respond to some visual conditions or change in visual conditions. In pilot work, I noticed that apparently sleeping babies opened their eyes abruptly in response to a rapid offset of light. In fact, one such observation has been replicated over and over again; the response to rapid offset of light is one of the most dramatic and easily demonstrable of all newborn visual behaviors.

These observations suggested two things. The first was that newborns are quite capable of responding to relatively small brightness shifts through their eyelids and, more than likely, to an absolute level of illumination. This fact should not have surprised us given the known transmittance characteristics of the eyelids; it has been standard procedure to examine evoked responses to bright strobe flashes in young infants as they sleep (for example, Ellingson, 1964). On the other hand, investigators have often ignored the potential influence of ambient light levels in investigations that focused on newborn responses to *non*visual stimulation. It is often reported, for example, that newborns respond to sound stimuli by clamping their eyelids shut (for example, Peiper, 1963; Pratt, 1954), the auro-palpebral response. However, research in our laboratory has shown that whether a newborn opens his/her eyes or clamps them depends on the ambient light level (Kearsley, 1973). Kearsley found that newborns opened their eyes (an orienting response) to mild tones when the room was dimly illuminated. Although he did not investigate the effects of light levels systematically, his pilot work agreed with findings of others that sounds presented under higher ambient light levels tended to produce lid clamping (a defensive response) even when the eyes were originally closed. These observations suggest that light levels should be considered in newborn research, especially when eye activity is used as an index of responsiveness. Additionally, the common use of eyelid opening as an indicator of state level should be qualified by a careful specification of light levels.

The second less obvious suggestion from our pilot observations was that the newborn might be equipped with a "rule" for opening eyes and looking *independent of the depth of sleep,* a rule that can be triggered by an appropriate visual signal. One characteristic of the light shift we had used for informal observations was that it occurred suddenly. On logical grounds, it would seem adaptive for the newborn to awaken, however briefly, in response to a sudden decrement in illumination; sudden darkening or shadowing elicits a fear or alerting response in many animals, presumably because it may signal the approach of a predator. The present study was carried out to investigate the effect of varying the suddenness of changes in ambient illumination levels on babies in alert or sleeping states.

The effect of rate of change of stimulus intensity has not been widely studied by infant researchers. Graham and Jackson (1970) reported unpublished studies by Kantowitz and Graham and by Jackson which employed an auditory stimulus with a 3 msec or 300 msec rise time to peak intensity. An increase in the time to reach maximum stimulus intensity was accompanied by an increase in the latency of the accelerative heart rate response to sound. Using rise times of much longer duration (2000 msec), Kearsley (1973) found rise time to tones to be an important variable in determining whether awake newborns responded with an orienting (eye opening and heart rate deceleration) or a defensive (eye closing and heart rate acceleration) pattern. To the best of my knowledge, no one has explored the effects of rise or fall time of visual input on newborn behavior, nor has anyone examined the effect of rise times as extended as that used in the study reported here (5000 msec).

The hypothesis was that sleeping newborns would respond with brief eye opening to rapid light offset but not to gradual light offset. I expected eye opening to rapid offset to be followed by closing, the idea being that if no danger were indicated, the baby would continue sleeping. On the other hand, I expected no response in sleeping babies to light *onset* whether the rise time was gradual or abrupt. There was no theoretical basis for what to expect in the awake newborns either for the rise time or onset-offset variable.

METHOD

Subjects. The babies were 32 newborns seen in the Cambridge Hospital laboratory. The data from 47 additional infants were not used because of experimental error ($n = 1$), equipment problems ($n = 5$), the babies did not meet criteria for either state group ($n = 22$), cried ($n = 5$), gagged ($n = 1$), or were coughing ($n = 1$).

Stimulus Materials. In this study only a white screen was used. With the tungsten stimulus lamps at full setting (approximately 50v) a reading of $3.08 \text{cd}/\text{m}^2$ was recorded. In all other respects the apparatus was identical to that of Study 1.

Procedure. The procedure for selecting infants from the nursery and for preparing them for the experiment was identical to Study 1.

Babies were in one of two state conditions: awake or asleep. (Since we observed rather than controlled state, babies were not literally *assigned* to the state conditions.) Which, if either, condition a baby was in depended on the visual activity during a 30-second baseline period. After a 180-second "rest" period for all subjects, the stimulus lights were extinguished gradually over a 5-7-second period. This was followed by 30 seconds of complete darkness. An "assignment"of the baby to the asleep group was made if the baby's eyes were closed for the last 10 seconds of this 30-second dark period. An"assignment" to the alert group was made if the baby's eyes were open for 20 or more of the 30 seconds, with at least 10 of these seconds consecutive. The criteria were not exhaustive; that is, it was possible for babies not to meet the criteria for either group. Since the experiment began immediately after the 30-second dark period, and dark-condition specifications precluded the monitoring of visual behavior, the experimenter could not know during the experiment which state group the baby would be in or if, in fact, the baby satisfied criteria for inclusion in either group.

Within the state-assignment conditions babies were assigned randomly to one of four groups, representing four combinations of onset-offset rate and light-dark sequence (see Fig. 4.1). Following the 30-second dark baseline period all babies received four 30-second light periods in alternation with four 30-second dark periods. For one-half the babies, the dark periods preceded the light periods; for the remaining babies, light periods preceded dark periods. For one-half of each of these stimulus-sequence subgroups the transition between light and dark was sudden; for the remaining babies the light-dark transition was quite gradual, taking place over a 5-7-second period. For all babies the post-transition periods were 30 seconds long, resulting in a somewhat longer experimental procedure (about 35-40 seconds) for the gradual- than for the sudden-transition groups.

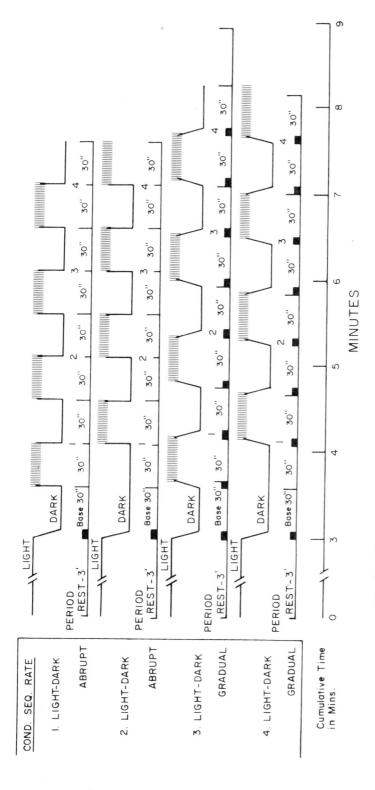

FIG. 4.1. Timing chart for the experimental conditions in Study 2. Intervals of transition, shown by solid squares, were not included in scoring of period. The transitions occurred over 5-7 sec. internals.

43

RESULTS

The measures used for this study were identical to those used in Study 1. The analysis of data was carried out by an observer who viewed the playback of the video-tape recording of the baby's eye. On separate occasions, the observer scored the baby's eye every 2.5 seconds (timed by metronome beat) on four measures: (1) degree of eye-opening; (2) degree of eye control; (3) sharpness of eye movements; and (4) size of eye movements. For each baby, 12 scores were recorded for each of eight periods for each of four variables. Analyses of these variables revealed striking replications of the results of Study 1 for awake infants. Babies opened their eyes widely in the dark and moved them actively. Once again, in darkness, the eyes were in control more frequently, eye movements were sharper and somewhat smaller than in light. The rate of transition from dark to light and vice versa did affect visual behavior, principally in the light condition. Babies opened their eyes more widely in the Abrupt-transition condition than in the Gradual-transition condition, but they maintained less control and had a lower percentage of sharp eye movements. Unfortunately, the "Asleep" Group remained, for the most part, asleep during the whole study, thus yielding few data of interest. The discussion of results will be organized around the four dependent measures taken on the Alert Group first. Then, data will be presented on the Asleep Group.

Alert Babies

Degree of Eye Opening. Degree of eye opening was judged along a four-point scale, as in Study 1 (see Fig. 3.2 for an illustration), as follows: 1 = eye closed completely, eyelids touching; 2 = lids open slightly (slitted) with iris mostly invisible; 3 = eye normally open, with whole pupil and most of iris visible; 4 = eyelids strained open, sometimes with white of eye visible above iris. These judgments were made fairly easily. Two scorers analyzed the same tape at the same time intervals and agreed perfectly on 106 judgments, disagreed by 1 category on 3 judgments, and by 2 categories on 1 judgment.

The surprising finding in Study 1 of a substantially greater percentage of category 4, open-to-strain judgments in darkness than light was replicated in the present study (in fact, within five percentage points for the light and dark conditions). Fully 56% of all judgments for time segments fell into category 4 when babies were in darkness, whereas only 12% fell in this category during light. Table 4.1 displays the percentage of all category judgments for the two light conditions.

The abrupt-transition rate also produced more category 4 assignments than the gradual rate (43% vs. 26%). Table 4.2 displays the percentage of all category judgments for the two transition rates.

TABLE 4.1
Percentage of Judgments in Four Degree of Eye-Open
Categories for the Dark and Light Conditions
for Study 2

Light Condition	Category			
	1	*2*	*3*	*4*
Light	28%	17%	43%	12%
Dark	14%	10%	20%	56%

An analysis of variance of the degree-of-opening score was carried out with Rate (of transition) as a between-subject variable and Condition (light-dark) and Number (of exposures) as within-subject variables in a 2 × 2 × 4 design. The datum for this analysis was the average of the 12 scores a baby received for a given 30-second period minus that baby's average baseline score.

The main effects of Condition, $F(1,14) = 28.68$, $p < .01$, and Number of Exposures, $F(3,42) = 22.23$, $p < .01$, were significant. Figure 4.2 displays the degree-of-eye-opening difference scores as a function of these factors and of the Rate factor. The largest effect was attributable to Light Condition with less opening in the light than in the dark. The next largest effect was produced by number of exposures with the scores in every condition decreasing with an increasing number of exposures.

This first analysis collapsed eye-opening scores over the time segments within a period. To examine the temporal response of the newborn to the Transition-Rate factor, an analysis was carried out on the first three scores (following the transition) in a period as a function of Condition, Rate, and the three Temporal Segments. The scores for both the Gradual- and the Abrupt-transition groups were the three scores (7.5 seconds of time) immediately following the time segment at which a steady illumination for that period had

TABLE 4.2
Percentage of Judgments in Four Degree of Eye-Open
Categories for the Sudden and Gradual Conditions in
Study 2

Light Condition	Category			
	1	*2*	*3*	*4*
Sudden	13%	9%	35%	43%
Gradual	30%	18%	27%	26%

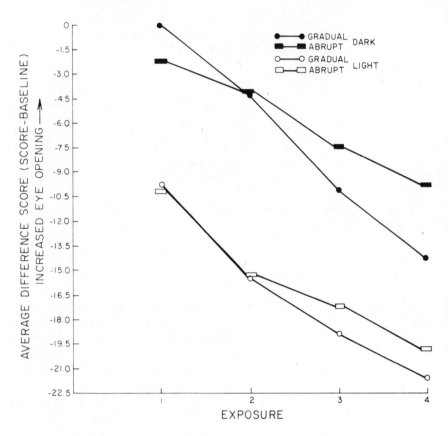

FIG. 4.2.   The effect of the dark and the light conditions, transition rate, and
number of exposures on average difference (from baseline) in eye opening in
Study 2.

been reached. This analysis, then, collapsed scores across the four exposures,
each subtracted from the score obtained during baseline.[1]

The Condition factor was the only stable main factor, $F(1,14) = 16.8$,
$p < .01$; additionally the Condition × Rate × Time interaction was marginally stable, $F(2,28) = 3.00, p < .10$). In accord with the prior analysis, the
scores for light conditions revealed less opening than for dark. The
Condition × Rate × Time interaction reflected more eye opening in the light

---

[1]There were only three transitions to darkness after the baseline period for babies in the
dark → light sequence. The first dark exposure for these subgroups followed the baseline period,
which was also dark, and thus no actual transition occurred at the beginning of their first dark
exposure. Therefore, the average of the scores obtained for each time segment for the other three
exposures was substituted. This same procedure was used for graphing scores in Fig. 4.3.

condition for the Abrupt than for the Gradual group. These relations are shown in Fig. 4.3 in the second panel of the figure. Also shown, in the first panel, are average scores during the gradual transition for the light-dark and dark-light transitions. As can be seen, these scores "tracked" the gradual shift in illumination. Finally, in the third panel is shown the combined total of the last three scores in the period. Although the light-dark difference was preserved, there was little difference as a function of transition rate except for a slight reversal that occurred in relative scores between the Abrupt-Light and Gradual-Light groups.

It is important to note that the Abrupt-Light Group had scores indicating more opening in the posttransition periods than the Gradual-Light Group; this comparison bears on the question of whether the greater opening of eyes in darkness than in light can be interpreted solely in terms of the effect of light level. If light level were the only factor operating, one would expect the opposite—more clamping of the eyes after an abrupt transition to light than after a gradual transition.

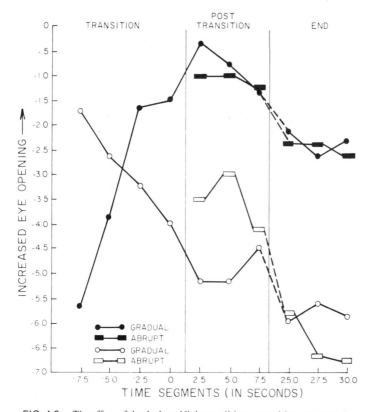

FIG. 4.3.   The effect of the dark and light conditions, transition rate, and time from transition on average difference (from baseline) in eye opening in Study 2.

Eye Control. Judgments of eye control were made for each baby by assigning each 2.5-second period a number indicating whether the eyes were closed, open and in control, or open and out of control. As for Study 1, the "out-of-control" assignment was made if, during any portion of the 2.5 second period, nystagmic eye movements occurred at either the temporal or nasal side of the eye. The majority of these movements occurred on the temporal side in groups of more than two. In a reliability check, 2 scorers each made 110 assignments based on the same video-tape record at the same time and disagreed on only 1.

The data were consistent with the prior study, as shown in Table. 4.3, which gives the percentage of in-control, out-of-control, and eye-closed assignments for the light-dark and gradual-abrupt breakdowns. Considering only those time segments in which the eyes were open, 18% of the light-condition judgments (92 of 510 judgments) were out-of-control, whereas, in dark, an out-of-control assignment was made only once in 622 judgments. This finding was not produced by a few babies only. Of the 16 babies, 13 had more out-of-control segments in light than in dark; for the remaining 3, no nystagmus was shown in any period. These results, then, replicate Study 1, which also revealed a substantially higher percentage of out-of-control eye movements in light than in dark—though the percentage of Study 1 was somewhat higher than in this study.

An additional finding of interest was the tendency for there to be significantly fewer out-of-control movements in light for babies in the Gradual condition than in the Abrupt condition (10% vs. 23%, excluding the eye-closed segments; $F[1,14] = 5.16$, $p < .05$).

The relation between out-of-control movements and time after the transition period is shown in Fig. 4.4. For both the Gradual- and Abrupt-Transition groups, the percentage of out-of-control movements was low in segment 1, highest in segment 2, and had returned to the original level by

TABLE 4.3

Percentage of Eye Movements in each of the Degree-of-Control Categories for the Dark and Light Conditions for the Two Transition Rates in Study 2

Light Condition	Rate of Change	Category		
		Eye Closed	*In-Control*	*Out-of-Control*
Light	Abrupt	21%	61%	18%
	Gradual	46%	48%	5%
Dark	Abrupt	12%	88%	0%
	Gradual	26%	74%	0%

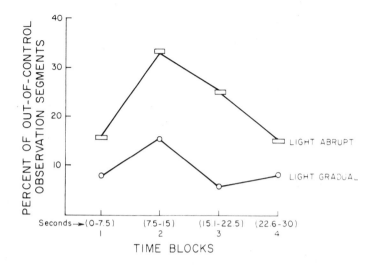

FIG. 4.4.   The effect of time from transition on percentage of out-of-control segments in light periods in Study 2. (Percentages are for eye-open segments only.)

segment 4. A large number of zero scores precluded a summary analysis of these data. However, the stability of this relation is demonstrated by the fact that 11 of 13 babies (who displayed any nystagmus at all) had their highest score in segment 2 ($n = 8$), or equaled their highest score in this segment ($n = 3$); the remaining 2 babies had their highest score in segments 1 and 4.

Type of Eye Movement.   Judgments of type of eye movement were made for those segments in which the eyes were open, moved, and were judged to be in control. Assignment was made to three categories: (1) sharp, jerky movements, usually with both the initiation and termination of the movement having an abrupt quality; (2) smooth, controlled movement, with initiation and termination definite but not jerky or abrupt; (3) slow drift, with initiation and termination somewhat indefinite or "sloppy." (This movement was slower than the jerky or controlled movements and more frequently had a vertical component.)

Two scorers made judgments of the type of movement variable for 114 segments and disagreed by 1 category on 11 segments and by 2 categories on 1. This measure yielded the lowest reliability of the various measures used in this study.

Table 4.4 shows the percentage of judgments in each category for the light-dark and gradual-abrupt conditions, and also the percentage of open-eye segments for which the eye did not move. Baseline differences between the Abrupt- and Gradual-Transition groups differed only slightly.

TABLE 4.4

Percentage of Judgments in Four Categories of Eye Movement for the Dark and Light Conditions and for the Two Rates of Change in Study 2

	Light Condition							
	Light				*Dark*			
Rate of Transition	*No Movement*	*Jerky*	*Smooth*	*Drift*	*No Movement*	*Jerky*	*Smooth*	*Drift*
Abrupt	15%	56%	18%	26%	8%	19%	62%	20%
Gradual	8%	43%	44%	13%	6%	20%	57%	24%

The most striking finding was the overall difference between light and dark conditions in the relation between jerky and smooth eye movements. In dark conditions, smooth movements were much more prevalent than jerky or drift movements (59.5%, 19.5%, and 22%, respectively), whereas, in light conditions jerky movements predominated over smooth movements (49.5% and 31%, respectively). This was one of the most stable findings of this study; 13 of 16 babies had sufficient data in both conditions for legitimate comparison. (Three babies in the gradual-light condition supplied fewer than 25% open-eye segments for judgment.) Not a single reversal of this trend (smooth movements in dark > light and jerky movements in light > dark) was noted, although one baby had an equal percentage of smooth eye movements in light and dark. These results replicated those of Study 1 in which a higher percentage of jerky movements and a lower percentage of smooth movements occurred in light than occurred in darkness.

Transition rate did not appear to affect dark behavior on the movement-type variable. However, there were indications that it affected light behavior differentially. The Abrupt-Transition condition produced a substantially lower percentage of smooth eye movements, and a higher percentage of drift and no movement, than the Gradual-Transition condition in light (18%, 26%, 15% vs. 44%, 13%, and 8%, respectively). The fact that three babies in the Gradual-Transition group did not contribute to these percentages makes statistical comparison somewhat difficult, but there was overlap of only one baby in the Gradual-Transition Group with any baby in the Abrupt-Transition Group. A t-test of these two groups on mean number of smooth movements was significant ($t = 2.51$, $p < .05$); however, given that these comparisons were post hoc, these results should be considered as suggestive rather than definitive.

However, it is interesting, that the Abrupt-Light Group produced a higher average eye-opening score but fewer smooth movements. The finding in both this study and Study 1 of more smooth eye movements in dark than in light might have been interpreted as reflecting the baby's higher state of activation in dark—a proposal supported by the higher degree of eye opening. Since the Abrupt-Transition Group could be expected to be more activated than the Gradual-Transition Group, their larger eye-opening scores fit with this interpretation. However, even though this group was probably more activated than its slow-rate counterpart, this group still produced more, not fewer, out-of-control eye movements and a lower percent of smooth movements. Thus, an activation-level interpretation can not explain all the results.

An additional indication that the Abrupt-Light condition produced unusual behavior is given by a within-subject comparison of percentage of no-eye-movement judgments. This group had about twice as many such judgments (15%) as the other three groups (about 8%). A median split for the

TABLE 4.5
Number of Subjects Above and Below Median on the
No-Movement Measure

	Abrupt	
	Light	Dark
+	7	1
−	1	7

same babies in the Light- and Dark-Abrupt groups on the no-movement variable is shown in Table 4.5 where it can be seen that 7 of 8 babies in the Abrupt-Transition groups had more no-movement scores in light than in dark. (See cautionary note in Chapter 3 concerning the interpretation of the "no-movement" category.)

Size of Eye Movement.   Judgments were made of size of eye movement for open and in-control segments every 2.5 seconds, as for the other dependent variables. Three categories were used: (1) large movement, in which the eye moved more than ¼ the diameter of the iris; (2) small movement, in which the eye movement was smaller than (1); (3) no movement, in which the eye was not observed to move. A reliability test on two observers revealed 8 disagreements in 112 judgments, all by one category.

Of all assignments made, 71% fell in the small movement category, 19% in the large movement, and 10%, no movement.

Table 4.6 gives a breakdown of mean percentage in each category for the Light-Dark and Abrupt-Gradual subgroups. Overall baseline differences between groups were slight and not taken into account.

The effect of light on this variable was fairly uniform for the two rate-of-transition groups. Subjects made a greater percentage of large movements

TABLE 4.6
Percentage of Judgments in Three Size-of-Movement Categories for the Dark and Light
Conditions and for the Two Transition Rates in Study 2

Rate of Transition	*Light Condition*					
	Light			*Dark*		
	No Movement	*Small Movement*	*Large Movement*	*No Movement*	*Small Movement*	*Large Movement*
Abrupt	15%	59%	26%	7%	81%	12%
Gradual	9%	57%	34%[a]	6%	81%	13%

[a]*Note.* Does not include three subjects.

during light periods than they did during dark periods, $F(1,12) = 11.41$, $p < .01$. This finding of a higher percentage of large movements in light than in dark (30% vs. 12%) replicates a similar but somewhat weaker (32% vs. 21%) difference obtained in Study 1. Rate of transition had no stable effect on the size-of-movement measure.

Asleep Babies

The Asleep Group was appropriately named. In each of four subgroups (the transition-rate and sequence combinations), only one of four babies had its eyes open for more than 1 of the 96 possible segments (2.5 seconds) of the experiment.

Inasmuch as newborns are thought to sleep almost all of the day (Wolff, 1959, estimated them to be in an alert, awake state approximately 10′ a day), it was surprising to note how difficult it was to obtain babies who met the criterion for assignment to this group. A review of the log book revealed that after four months of attempts to carry out the study, one-half the subjects had been observed. Ten of these fell in the Alert category and only six in the Asleep category. Fully 17 babies had not been included by this point either because they had not met criterion for either group or because of problems associated only with awake newborns (that is, poor camera contrast, crying, or the baby moved too much). These findings are astonishing in view of the fact that all a baby need do to be included in the asleep group was keep his/ her eyes closed for 10 continuous seconds during 20 seconds in dark after a 180-second rest period in light. Our own difficulty in obtaining "awake" babies for the studies of form scanning (to be described later) suggests either that light puts babies to sleep or darkness wakes them up. The tendency for babies to awaken in darkness fits with our informal experience and is probably reflected in these data.

Thus, our criterion for considering a baby to be asleep may have been too stiff. A baby who keeps his/ her eyes closed in darkness within 1½ hours prior to a feeding, may be in very deep sleep (possibly still somewhat affected by anesthesia) and unresponsive to mild stimulus inputs.

There is negative evidence, then, on our hypothesis that newborn infants *in any state* will respond to rapid offset of medium-intensity light. However, it may be true that newborns who are not in the deepest level of sleep (or not anesthetized) would be sensitive to the rate of light offset.

DISCUSSION

The results of this study strongly confirmed those of Study 1 on all four dependent variables. For the degree-of-eye opening variable, there were more category 4 assignments in darkness than in light and more eye opening in general. There were substantially more out-of-control segments in light than in darkness, more jerky movements, and fewer smooth movements. Additionally, more large movements were made in the Light condition than in the Dark condition. All of these results replicated those of Study 1.

The results were less informative with regard to our interest in the effect of rate of transition on awake and sleeping babies. Asleep babies remained asleep despite our visual stimulus manipulations. Either I was simply wrong in suggesting that rapid light offset would arouse a sleeping newborn, or the principle must be qualified. It may be the case that the criteria for a baby's inclusion in the Asleep Group were too demanding. If so, then newborns do not sleep as deeply or as much as the literature suggests, or darkness awakens those who, in light, might be judged to be asleep. At any rate, it is clear that for the level of light intensity used in this experiment, light offset did not arouse babies regardless of state.

The other qualification may relate to the intensity factor. The illumination level of the white screen with the stimulus light set at maximum intensity was 3.08 cd/m^2. According to Haber and Hershenson (1973, p. 14) this is only slightly more illumination than that of white paper reflecting the light from a full moon and certainly less than the illumination required for comfortable reading. That the intensity was quite low is indicated by the post-transition eye opening measure that revealed more eye opening to an abrupt than gradual transition from dark to light. Thus, it may be that the offset of a relatively low light level was simply not enough to stir the heavily sleeping newborn.

The transition-rate variable did affect the behavior of Awake babies. Babies appeared to maintain a more awake state in the Abrupt-Transition condition than in the Gradual-Transition condition. Overall, their eye-opening scores were higher and declined less from the baseline levels over multiple exposures than they did for the Gradual-Rate Group (Fig. 4.2). Additionally, the post-transition eye-opening scores (Fig. 4.3) suggested a more positive response by the Abrupt-Rate Group to light onset.

One might argue that the difference found between the Dark and Light conditions simply reflected more arousal in newborns in darkness. The degree-of-eye-opening measure is consistent with this interpretation; an abrupt transition to light could be expected to arouse the newborn and, from this argument, should parallel the Dark-condition data in producing more eye opening. It did. However, the Abrupt-Light condition also elicited significantly more nystagmus and fewer smooth movements, relations which are opposite to those we have found for light-dark comparisons. Thus, both darkness and abruptness may increase arousal, but the similarity for eye opening must be considered in relation to dissimiliarities in the qualitative nature at eye movements. Arousal can not be the whole story, and, additionally, it is fair to add that the dependent variables did not index identical processes.

Yet another finding deserves comment. I argued from the data of Study 1 that the eye-opening measure was not simply an indicator of brightness of light. However, the plot of average degree of eye opening during the transition from light to dark and from dark to light in Fig. 4.3 for the Gradual-Transition groups reveals a smooth and consistent "tracking" by this measure of the light intensity change. I do not deny that light intensity affects the degree of eye opening in newborns. What I am claiming, based on the finding in Study 1 that a substantial difference in screen brightness had virtually no effect on eye opening, and the finding in Study 2 that gradual onset of light produced more eye opening than abrupt onset, is that intensity is not the *sole* determinant. Relatively speaking, the Abrupt condition should have momentarily increased the subjective light intensity and produced eye closing.

At this point then, the rule system might look like this:

1. If in deep sleep, ignore onset and offset of mild light regardless of rate of change.

2. If in moderate sleep, respond only to light which changes abruptly. (This is an hypothesis, not a rule with any support at this time.)

3. If awake, and light not too bright, open eyes.

4. If in darkness, initiate a controlled (by internally organized instructions), detailed search for subtle shadows or edges.

5. If in light, initiate a broad uncontrolled search for edges.

Since (1) and (2) are tentative, they will be exlcuded from further discussion.

The following experiment proceeds one step further in the complexity of the visual situation to examine how babies deal with a spatial brightness transition or contour in their visual field.

5

Study 3,
How Newborns Scan an Edge:
Newborn Visual Scanning
of Equally Detectable
Vertical and Horizontal Edges

Studies 1 and 2 were concerned with the effects of light and darkness on newborn scanning in the absence of visual form. This study concerns what newborn babies do when they confront the most simple visual pattern: a black-white linear edge.

Earlier studies, relevant to the present one, were carried out in Kessen's laboratory at Yale University. Salapatek and Kessen (1966) presented a black equilateral triangle to newborns and recorded visual fixations. For control purposes, they also presented a homogeneous black screen. As compared to the control stimulus, the triangle produced a tighter clustering of fixations and a marked shift in average position of the eye in the visual field that was closer to the triangle's location. Most striking was the newborn's tendency to scan near only one angle of the triangle. Several questions were raised by these findings including whether or not linear edges as well as angles could attract the newborn's gaze and whether or not fixation clustering was uniquely produced by angles or was a general characteristic of newborn scanning over any visual form.

Kessen et al. (1972) addressed these questions by showing newborns an even more elementary form, a linear, black-white edge similar to those used in the present study. Newborns were shown a vertical edge (left or right of field center) and a horizontal edge (above or below center), separately, in alternation with a blank control field. Vertical stimuli, as in the Salapatek and Kessen study, affected the average fixation position of the eye; the average eye location was closer to the location of the edge and, in addition, the edge region was crossed more when the edge was actually present. There was no effect on the clustering of visual fixations, so it is clear that not all patterns constrain scanning. This is a point I pursue in a later chapter as it will be important for my interpretation of the factors that control newborn scanning. The most surprising result of this study, however, was that the horizontal edge had no effect on scanning at all, the babies behaving as though they did not see it.

The finding of strong vertical-edge attraction but no horizontal-edge attraction was intriguing in its own right. But it also hinted at the possibility of a general principle at work in newborn scanning of any visual form and, thus, seemed worthy of pursuit. Before stating the two interesting hypotheses of the vertical-horizontal difference I make obeisance to parsimony and consider a possible interpretation which I do not believe. Newborns characteristically move their eyes much more along the horizontal than the vertical axis. Although this is true of primates at all ages, the difference is much more striking in the newborn. Since the edges used in the Kessen et al. study were displaced from the center of the visual field by about 17° (7.62 cm above, below, left, or right), the normal horizontal-scanning activity of newborns made it more likely that they would find the vertical than the horizontal edge. The reason this interpretation seems implausible to me is that newborns frequently approached, even crossed, the horizontal edge location, but did so no more during experimental periods when the edge was there than during control periods when it was not. We might have expected less attractiveness of the horizontal edge than the vertical edge but not an absence of any effect at all. However, the one merit of this interpretation is that it considers stimulus attractiveness to be a joint function of the newborn's scanning ability and the formal aspects of the stimulus, not only a function of the stimulus alone; this point I gladly concede.

The second interpretation assumes that scanning activity reflects the facts of visual neurophysiology. The presence of simple-cell analyzers for edges and lines in the striate cortex has been well documented in cats and primates (for example, Hubel & Wiesel, 1959, 1968), even in the earliest days of life (Hubel & Wiesel, 1963; Wiesel & Hubel, 1974), although the relative maturity of orientation analyzers has been questioned (Barlow & Pettigrew, 1971; Pettigrew, 1974). If newborns do possess line detectors it could be argued that the scanning data from Kessen et al. suggest that vertical-edge detectors are present at birth but not horizontal-edge detectors. If so, the perceptual world of the newborn would be strange, indeed, and such a state of affairs would have strong implications for a theory of perceptual development in early infancy. There are no data supporting differential density of horizontal- and vertical-edge operators at birth in newborn monkeys or cats (Hubel & Wiesel, 1962; Pettigrew, 1974; Wiesel & Hubel, 1974). An additional problem with this and the first interpretation is that they address only the question of why vertical edges were more attractive than horizontal edges. Neither addresses questions of why newborn scanning takes the form it does with an effective stimulus—why newborns cross edges when they find them, why their fixations cluster around one angle of a triangle, and so on. We would do well to seek an explanation that not only accounts for the attractiveness findings but which also permits generalization to a broader range of visual activity and visual stimuli.

A third interpretation concerns not whether the vertical and horizontal edges were found, nor whether one could be seen better than the other, but, rather, what the baby could do with them. The tendency for newborns to cross edges when they find them is revealing. Although I am anticipating the argument to be made in Chapter 9, it is reasonable to assume that eye movements which cross contours also create strong effects on visual cortical firing because the edge is successively relocated on different parts of the retina, near the fovea, a region that contains a high density of retinal receptors. The reason that vertical edges may have been attractive is that horizontal edgecross eye movements near the edge were easily made with resulting consequences on cortical-firing rate. On the other hand, because vertical eye movements are so difficult for the newborn, the offset horizontal edges, perhaps near the limit of controllable vertical excursions, may have been very difficult to cross. If this reasoning is correct, then the vertical-horizontal difference implies much more than an empirical fact. Babies may be wired to locate contrast regions that are easily crossable and to stay away from ones that are not. This possibility has several implications: for newborn scanning of any visual form, for the interplay between stimulus features and the newborn's motor capabilities in controlling information-seeking behavior, and for the role that neurophysiological activity may play in systematic visual routines that we have seen. I pursue these matters further in Chapter 9.

This study and Study 4 were carried out to examine the three possible interpretations of the vertical-horizontal difference. In this study, vertical and horizontal edges were shown to newborns, but their location was at the predicted resting location of the eye based on the data of the Kessen et al. study. This resting or average location was about 7° to the right of the center of the visual field and about 6° below it. The manipulation should have made the edges maximally "findable" and maximally "crossable" for either of the two orientations. If the "detectability" (visual analyzer) interpretation is correct, the horizontal edge should still not affect scanning in any way. If the "findability" interpretation is correct, newborns should stay nearer the location of the horizontal edge in experimental as opposed to control trials. However, there is no reason to expect that more crossings of that location should occur or that the nature of scanning should change. If the "crossability" interpretation is correct, newborns should not only stay near the horizontal as well as the vertical edge, they should also make attempts to cross over it.

METHOD

Subjects. Sixteen normal, full-term awake newborn infants, between 24 and 96 hours of age, born at the Cambridge Hospital served as subjects. The data from numerous other infants were not used because they fell asleep or cried (n = 33), did not meet age or normality criteria (n = 3), moved too much or did not photograph well (n = 7), the equipment malfunctioned (n = 6), or for miscellaneous reasons (e.g., experimenter error, n = 12).

Apparatus and Stimuli. The eye-recording apparatus was described in Chapter 2. Stimuli were prepared by spraying paint onto window screening mounted in an aluminum frame 50.8 cm × 50.8 cm. Six stimulus screens were prepared as described in Chapter 2; these are shown in Fig. 5.1:

1. VB—a screen with a vertical boundary 3.18 cm to the right of field center with the large section black
2. VW—as (1) but with the large section white
3. HB—a screen with a horizontal boundary 2.54 cm below field center with the large section black
4. HW—as (3) with the large section white
5. BC—a homogenous black (control) screen
6. WC—a homogeneous white (control) screen.

The positions of the vertical and horizontal edges were based on predictions of the "resting" location of the baby's eye during control periods; these predictions were based, in turn, on a calculation of the average fixation

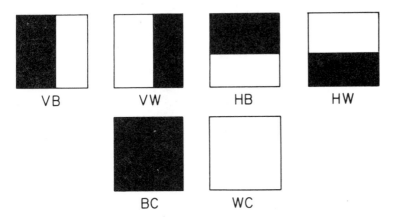

FIG. 5.1. The stimulus screens used in Study 3.

position during scanning of homogeneous visual fields in the Kessen et al. study.

Screens were slid into position approximately 24.13 cm from the infant's eye. The light readings on the screens were as follows: white portions = 3.98-7.20 cd/m^2, black portions = .51-1.03 cd/m^2, and black-white boundary = 2.06 cd/m^2.

A white 10.16 cm × 15.24 cm index card was mounted horizontally above a wooden stand by a machine bolt. The stand was located behind the baby's head. The card, approximately 2.54 cm above the baby's eyes, was rotated to obscure the newborn's vision of the screen while it was being changed.

Procedure.   An awake open-eyed infant was selected from the newborn nursery before the midday feeding. All infants were seen between 11:30 AM and 1:00 PM. The experimenter swaddled the infant and placed him on a padded board that contained a vertical padded hip and head plates on either side and served to constrain lateral body and head movement. A Telfa gauze pad was placed over the infant's left eye. The platform was slid into position so that the eye was centered in the field of the TV camera. When picture quality and head position were optimized, the experimenter started the polygraph, the audio-tape recorder, and the video-tape recorder, and the experiment began.

During the experiment, infants were presented a sequence of 5 stimulus screens in the following time sequence: (1) control screen—30 seconds; (2) experimental screen—60 seconds; (3) control screen—30 seconds; (4) experimental screen—60 seconds; (5) control screen—30 seconds.

The particular experimental and control screens a baby saw depended on which of 4 groups the subject had been assigned to, as follows: (1) HVB—horizontal edge first (period 2), vertical screen second (period 4), with both screens containing the large portion black; (2) VHB—same as (1), but the order of presentation of vertical and horizontal screens was reversed; (3) HVW—same as (1), but the large portion was white; (4) VHW—same as (2), but the large portion was white. Control screens for each group were always the same brightness as the largest portion of the experimental stimuli.

After each period the experimenter rotated the index card over the infant's eye to obscure his/her view. The stimulus screen was slid out and a new one slid in, a procedure requiring 15-20 seconds. Then the index card was removed and a new period commenced. The prescribed time periods were not adhered to rigidly. The goal was to obtain good scoreable data for 60 seconds during experimental periods and for 30 seconds during control periods. If an infant moved his head so that the position of his eye was out of the camera field, or closed his eyes, extra time was added to compensate. The experimenter kept track of time by referring to a running clock.

Infants were permitted to suck on a pacifier throughout the experiment, a manipulation that decreased head movement and increased the likelihood of keeping the infant in an awake, nonfretful state. A second experimenter held the pacifier from the infant's right side and also adjusted the side IR light when necessary.

RESULTS

The analyses of the ocular fixation data may be conveniently subdivided into analyses of eye position and analyses of eye movement. Three independent variables were involved in the analyses to be described: Brightness (B—black or white larger portion of the field with black or white control screen, respectively). Sequence (S—edge presented in a vertical-horizontal order or vice versa), and Condition (C—experimental or control period). In the mixed-mode analyses, the B and S factors were between-subject variables, whereas the C factor was a within-subject variable.[1] Each control-period measure was comprised of the average of the control period preceding and the control period following the relevant 60-second experimental period. Analyses were carried out separately to examine the effect of vertical and horizontal edges.

The analysis of the fixation data revealed that the newborns' average fixation position was nearer the edge location when the edge was actually there than when it was not. This relation held for both the vertical and horizontal orientations. The newborns' scanning was slightly more constrained along the axis perpendicular to the stimulus orientation during experimental periods. However, they scanned much more broadly along the axis parallel to the horizontal edge when the edge was presented than during control periods.

Analyses of eye movements revealed somewhat larger eye movements when the stimuli were presented, the major effect being on the X-axis component of movement. Additionally, infants crossed the edge location more when the edge was there than when it was not for both orientations. A very interesting relation was also found for both orientations when the size of eye movements that crossed the edge location was compared for experimental and control conditions. During experimental conditions, these eye movements were substantially larger than during control conditions; virtually no difference was found for movements that did not cross the edge location. Details follow in the next section.

---

[1]The appropriate nonpooled within-subject error terms were used to evaluate all within-subject main effects and interactions.

Analyses of Eye Position and Disperson

Vertical Edge.   An analysis of the average horizontal distance of fixation from the vertical edge revealed a stable C effect, $F(1,12) = 10.5, p < .01$, with subjects closer to the edge on experimental than on control trials (2.41 cm vs. 6.02 cm, respectively). The predicted resting location of the eye on the X axis during control periods, 3.18 cm to the right of center, was close to the observed position, 3.94 cm to the right of center. Figure 5.2 shows a frequency distribution of fixations on the X axis over the field for control and experimental trials. "Regions" of 7.62 cm were defined around the edge with the actual edge located in the center of Region 5. One can see a clear increase in number of fixations in Region 5 (51% of all fixations) during experimental periods in comparison to the control periods (36% for all fixations), $F(1,12) = 10.1, p < .01$.

An ANOVA of the average variance in distribution of fixations on the X axis revealed only a slightly smaller variance in experimental periods than control periods. A slight, nonsignificant, increase in variance along the Y axis was found in experimental periods.

Horizontal Edge.   An analysis of average vertical distance of fixation from the horizontal edge revealed a stable C effect, $F(1,12) = 5.6, p < .05$, with fixation closer to the edge region during experimental than control periods (2.16 vs. 3.45 cm). This finding suggests that the detectability interpretation of the Kessen et al. (1972) study was wrong. There was also a stable B effect as well as a B × C interaction. The B and BC effects were

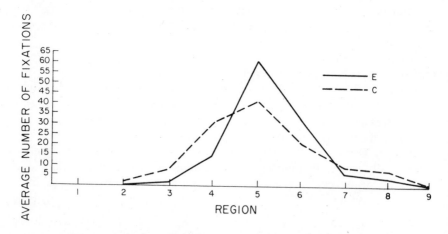

FIG. 5.2.   Frequency distribution of fixations across regions for experimental and control periods for vertical edges in Study 3. (The regions each represent 7.62 cm width in the real field with the edge lying in the center of Region 5.)

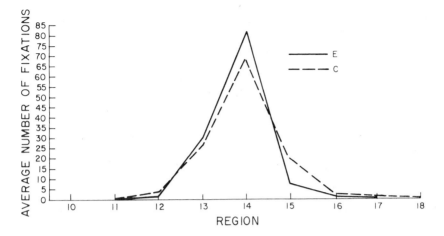

FIG. 5.3.   Frequency distribution of fixations across regions for experimental and control periods for horizontal edges in Study 3. (The regions each represent 7.62 cm height in the real field with the edge lying in the center of Region 14.)

attributable to control-period data; for ₁ne black large-field group the average distance from the edge location was extremely small, 1.35 cm, whereas for the white-field large group the distance was large, 5.59 cm. A similar explanation accounts for a S × C interaction with sequence 1 subjects closer during control periods than sequence 2 subjects (2.36 vs. 2.77 cm). The observed position of the eye during control periods was 3.00 cm below center, not far from the predicted position of 2.54 cm below center. Figure 5.3 displays a frequency distribution of fixations over the field along the Y axis. Again, parallel regions of 7.62 cm in width were defined around the horizontal edge with the actual edge located at the center of region 14. An increase in number of fixations in this region occurred during experimental periods; 68% of all fixations fell in region 14 during experimental periods, whereas 58% were in this region during control periods. This difference was stable, $F(1,12) =$ 10.5, $p < 0.01$, but was again complicated by B and B × C and S × C factors.

Similar to the vertical-edge conditions, there was a slight, albeit nonsignificant, decrease in variance along the perpendicular Y axis, which occurred from control to experimental periods. However, in contrast to the vertical-edge condition, there was a striking increase in variance along the X (parallel) axis from control to experimental periods (10.59 and 17.96 cm, respectively; $F(1,12) = 7.97$, $p < .05$).

Data on location and distribution, then, revealed that subjects fixated, on the average, nearer the edge position when either the horizontal or vertical edge was actually present rather than when it was not. Presentations of only the horizontal edge affected the distribution of fixations, strikingly increasing the distribution along the parallel (X) axis. This is the first time a stimulus has been found to increase fixation distribution; previous studies have reported either that a stimulus produces fixation clustering (Salapatek & Kessen, 1966) or that it has no effect at all (Kessen et al., 1972).

Analyses of Eye Movements

Vertical Edge. Eye movements were somewhat larger during experimental periods when the vertical edge was shown than during corresponding control periods, but an analysis of size of eye movement revealed no stable effect. A marginal difference was found in movement along the X axis alone,[2] $F(1,12) = 3.8$, $p < .10$ with larger movements during experimental periods, but no difference was found on the Y axis alone. The average size of the X-axis component of eye movement for control and experimental periods was 2.34 and 2.67 cm, respectively.

An analysis of percentage of movements that crossed the edge revealed a reliably greater percentage of crosses[3]—$F(1,12) = 24.4$, $p < .001$—during experimental as opposed to control periods (10.6% vs. 21.3%, respectively). A B effect, not of any interest, was also stable with large black-field subjects crossing more than large white-field subjects. Although the finding of a greater number of edge crosses during experimental periods appears to confirm a "crossability" interpretation, for at least the vertical-edge orientation, there is a criticism of my reasoning that precludes using crossing data alone for confirmation. The increased crossing during experimental periods may be an artifact of the fixation data. These data indicated that newborns stay nearer the edge during experimental than during control periods; increased crossing of an edge might be expected if the infant were closer to it. This could happen if, say, the newborn were programmed to make 3.3 to 3.6 cm eye movements each half second even if the infant were in a "random walk," because the baby was closer to the edge region during experimental periods.

To determine whether or not the increase in edge crosses during experimental periods reflected more than simple proximity and random movement, an analysis was carried out to examine whether eye movements that crossed the edge region were different in any way from those that did not. A "random walk" interpretation would predict that there would be no difference. The size of eye movements was examined separately for eye movements that crossed

---

[2]A noninterpretable BC interaction was found for size of X movements.

[3]Successive frames on which there was no movement were not included.

TABLE 5.1
Average Size of Eye Movement (cm) for Experimental
and Control Periods and for Each Movement Type for
Vertical Edges in Study 3

	Movement Type	
Period	Cross	No Cross
Experimental	6.10	3.02
Control	4.88	3.18

the edge region and for those that did not cross the edge region for control and experimental periods. Table 5.1 displays the size of eye movement as a function of both condition and movement type.[4]

An analysis of variance identical to those described above with Type (T; cross vs. no cross) added as a within-subject variable revealed a significant C × T interaction, $F(1,112) = 6.8, p < .05$. As might be expected, the C main effect was also stable, $F(1,12) = 33.3, p < .001$, with cross movements larger than no-cross movements. (One would expect that the larger the eye movement the higher the likelihood that any region would be crossed, including the edge region. Thus, it is the greater difference between cross and no-cross movements during experimental rather than control periods that is important.) It is important to note the similarity in average size of no-cross movements during the control and experimental periods which differed only by 0.15 cm; babies did not simply make larger eye movements during experimental periods, nonselectively. The interaction effect was clearly produced by an increase in size of cross movements during experimental periods; these were 25% larger than those during control periods.

Horizontal Edge. Eye movements were somewhat larger during experimental periods when the horizontal edge was shown than during corresponding control periods (3.56cm vs. 3.23 cm). An analysis of variance revealed a marginally stable effect of the C factor ($p < .10$). As for the vertical edges, there was a marginal increase for size of movement along the X axis— $F(1,12) = 3.8, p < .10$—with moves larger during experimental periods. There was no stable effect for the Y axis alone.

An analysis of percentage of movements that crossed the edge produced a marginal C effect—$F(1,12) = 4.5, p < .10$—with subjects crossing more during experimental (26.2%) than control (19.6%) periods. The B effect was

---

[4]These figures for size of eye movement appear larger than those described above. It should be remembered that the table entries are averages for given types of eye movements; many more no-cross movements were made during all periods which resulted in a smaller overall average.

TABLE 5.2
Average Size of Eye Movement (cm) for Experimental
and Control Periods and for Each Movement Type for
Horizontal Edges in Study 3

	Movement Type	
Period	Cross	No Cross
Experimental	5.28	3.15
Control	4.57	3.05

stable ($p < .05$), with the black-large condition producing more edge crosses, probably as a result of the greater proximity to edge during the control periods (as described in the fixation data discussed earlier). During control periods, 28.1% of movements crossed the edge in this condition as opposed to 17.7% in the white condition. A noninterpretable S × C interaction was also found.

An analysis of size of eye movement as a function of type of movement comparable to that described for the vertical condition was carried out. Table 5.2 displays the average eye movement as a function of period and type—cross vs. no-cross.

As with the vertical edge, there was a stable T × C interaction, $F(1,12) = 6.4$, $p < .05$; no-cross movements were quite similar for experimental and control periods differing by about .10 cm whereas, the experimental cross movements were approximately 16% largeer than control cross movements. As with the vertical edges, there was also a stable C effect with cross movements were approximately 16% larger than control cross movements. interaction ($p < .05$).

The eye movement data, then, suggest an effect on edge crosses of both horizontal and vertical edges. Good correspondence was also found for the size-of-movement data. There was a marginal effect on overall size of movement, collapsing across cross and no-cross movements along the X axis for both edge orientations. In addition, when the type of movement was considered (that is, whether or not the movement crossed the edge), there was clear agreement for both edge orientations that cross movements in experimental periods were differentially larger than no-cross movements when compared to the difference for control periods.

DISCUSSION

The present study produced confirmation of earlier work in several respects. The vertical edge clearly attracted the newborn's gaze and, in addition, produced a substantial number of contour crosses; both of these findings confirmed earlier work (Kessen et al., 1972). However, the earlier study reported no effect of horizontal edges at all, on fixation position, distribution of fixations or number of edge crosses. The present findings deny the possibility that newborns lack horizontal edge detectors. Furthermore, the effect of vertical and horizontal edges both on average fixation position and on number of contour crosses supports the crossability interpretation of the earlier Kessen et al. study. This interpretation was strengthened by the finding that eye movements that crossed the edge region were larger when the edge was actually there than when it was not—a clear denial of a "random walk" interpretation of the increase in contour crossings.

One of the surprises of the present study was the increase in scan variance along the X axis when a horizontal edge was presented. It seemed possible that a similar results might have been overlooked in the analyses of the Kessen et al. study. A reanalysis of these data showed this not to be the case. In fact, variance along the X axis in that study was slightly *smaller* during experimental than during control periods. The present finding of increased X variance seems related to the increase in the average size of movement along the X axis, but this is not a necessary relationship; average size of eye movement along the X axis also increased when a vertical edge was shown (from control to experimental trials), but X-axis variance actually decreased. The larger eye movements and greater X-axis variance, apparently, reflected attempts by the newborn to cross the horizontal edge within the constraints of his/her poor control over vertical movements. Given a shallow Y slope, the likelihood of crossing a horizontal edge is increased through an increase in the length of the X vector.

Further discussion of the findings from this study will be delayed until after the next study is presented. The next study confirmed the important findings of this study, whereas the nuisance factors were not replicated.

6

Study 4
How Newborns Scan a Bar:
Newborn Visual Scanning
of Equally Crossable
Vertical and Horizontal Bars

The present experiment was designed and carried out before results were analyzed from Study 3 (alas, the fate of technically demanding research on newborns for which findings are sometimes not available until the subject is almost old enough to read about them).

I was doubtful that simple relocation of the horizontal edge to an optimal position for crossing in Study 3 would eliminate the differences in appeal of the horizontal and vertical edges. My reasoning was as follows. Given that the cortical stimulation arising from an edge crossing is what keeps a baby near an edge, and given that horizontal eye movements are more easily generated than vertical eye movements, the "action-stimulus" combination should prove an advantage for vertical stimuli. I did not anticipate that Study 3 would be so effective in eliminating vertical-horizontal contour differences in scanning or that the newborn would find an apparent solution to the horizontal-edge problem—increasing the X vector of eye movement and dispersion to compensate for a limited Y vector and range. At a minimum, though, the present study, which dealt with bars rather than edges, provided a replication of the results of Study 3 as Study 2 did of Study 1. Clearly, replication attempts are rare in psychological research in general, and even rarer in newborn research; results comparable to those of Study 3 would substantially increase our confidence in them, as did the replication of Study 1 by Study 2.

The goal of this experiment was to equate the "firing potential" of horizontal and vertical stimuli by designing them in a way that would compensate for differences between the horizontal and vertical vectors of eye movement; i.e., to equate the result of the "action-stimulus" combination for

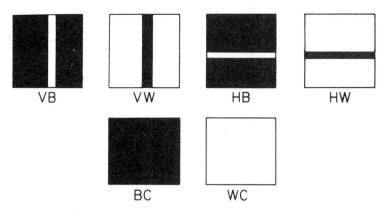

FIG. 6.1. The stimulus screens used in Study 4.

the two orientations. Vertical and horizontal bars of differing width were prepared to equate for the likelihood that babies would cross the contours (see Fig. 6.1). Since more movement normally occurs along the horizontal than vertical axis, the vertical bar was made wider than the horizontal bar. I reasoned that if the centers of the bars were placed in the predicted average resting location of the eye, the differences in likelihood of crossing one or the other edges of the bars would be at least partially compensated. The actual width of the bars was a function of the predicted dispersion of fixations along the axis perpendicular to each bar. By "standardizing" the width of the bars against the expected dispersion of fixations on the perpendicular axis, I hoped that newborns would have a roughly equal likelihood of crossing either side of the bars in the two orientations.[1] Accordingly, the vertical bar was one standard deviation of predicted dispersion along the horizontal axis, and the horizontal, narrower, bar was one standard deviation of predicted dispersion along the vertical axis.

METHOD

Subjects. Sixteen normal, full-term awake newborns (born at the Cambridge Hospital) between 24 and 96 hours of age served as subjects in the present study. The data from several other infants were not used because they fell asleep or cried (n = 19), did not meet age or normality criteria (n = 7),

---

[1]Of course this reasoning holds only on the average. The predicted location and dispersion were averages, not measures based on the particular infants involved. Additionally, it is an actual movement that produces an edge cross not some derivative of a dispersion measure. Still, the dispersion metric seemed like a reasonable one to try first.

moved too much or did not photograph well (n = 5), because equipment malfunctioned (n = 3), or for miscellaneous reasons (for example, experimenter error, n = 9).

Apparatus. The apparatus, room, noise level, and lighting were as identical to that in Study 3 as possible.

Stimuli. The stimuli were spray painted onto 50.8 × 50.8 cm screens in the same manner as described in Chapter 2. Four screens were prepared: (1) VB—a black screen with a white vertical bar 6.67 cm wide centered 3.18 cm to the right of center; (2) VW—as (1), but with a black vertical bar on a white field; (3) HB—a black screen with a white horizontal bar 3.81 cm in width whose center was 2.54 cm below field center; and (4) HW—as (3), but with a black bar on a white field. For control periods a homogeneous white field was used when the experimental-period bar was black (conditions 2 and 4), and a black field was used when the experimental-period bar was white.

Light readings of screens were as follows: 3.98-7.20 cd/m^2 on the white portion; .51-1.03 cd/m^2 on the black portion, and 3.25 cd/m^2 on the borders.

Procedure. All procedural details were as identical to those in Study 3 as possible.

RESULTS

As with Study 3, the results are described first in terms of eye-position data and then in terms of eye-movement data. The between-subject variables in the analyses of variance were, once again, Brightness (B) and Sequence (S), and the within-subject variable was Condition (C). Analyses were carried out on the effects of vertical bars and horizontal bars separately.

The results of this study paralleled those of Study 3 quite closely for the interesting variables, whereas the significant nuisance outcomes were not replicated. Newborns' average fixation position was closer to the center of the horizontal and vertical bars during experimental than during control periods. Again, the dispersion of fixations during experimental periods was only slightly more constrained than during control periods along the axis perpendicular to the orientation of the bar. The horizontal-axis distribution once again increased strikingly when the horizontal bar was presented.

As before, larger eye movements were found during experimental than control periods with the major effect on the X-axis component; for the horizontal bar, this effect was stable. The number of eye movements that crossed at least one of the bar contours was greater during experimental than control periods. Finally, the interesting interaction between Type of eye movement and Period, obtained in Study 3, replicated for both bar orientations. That is, eye movements that crossed the location of a bar contour were differentially large during experimental periods. More detail is provided in the following.

Analyses of Eye Position and Dispersion

Vertical Bar. An analysis of average perpendicular distance of fixation from the *center* of the bar revealed a stable C effect ($F(1,12) = 8.7, p < .05$), with subjects closer to bar center during experimental than during control trials (1.80 vs. 4.34 cm, respectively). A stable B × S × C interaction reflected a smaller difference during control periods, in one of the four BS subgroups than in the other three; however, in all four subgroups, babies were closer to the edge during experimental than control trials. The observed eye position during control periods was 4.98 cm to the right of center, somewhat further from the predicted location—of 3.18 cm—than in the edge study. Figure 6.2 shows a frequency distribution of fixations on the X axis over the field for control an experimental trials. Regions of 7.62 cm were defined around the center of the vertical bar with bar center coinciding with the center of region 5 (see Fig. 6.2). There was a clear increase in average number of fixations in Region 5 from control to experimental trials with 64% of all experimental fixations falling in that region as opposed to 50% of all control fixations $F(1,12) = 17.0, p < .01$.

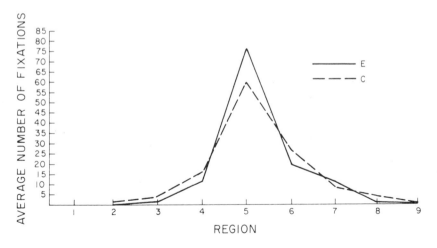

FIG. 6.2.   Frequency distribution of fixations across regions for experimental and control periods for vertical bars in Study 4. (The regions each represent 7.62 cm width in the real field with the bar center lying in the center of Region 5.)

An ANOVA on the variance in distribution of fixations revealed, as in the edge study, a slight nonsignificant decrement (from control to experimental periods) in distribution of fixations along the perpendicular, X, axis and a slight nonsignificant increment along the Y axis.

Horizontal Bar.   An ANOVA of distance from the center of the horizontal bar on the perpendicular Y axis revealed no stable effect; however, as in Study 3, the average distance of fixations from the center of the bar was smaller during experimental than control periods (3.02 and 4.47 cm, respectively). The observed Y position of the eye during control periods was 1.96 cm below center, not far from the predicted location of 2.54 cm below center. Figure 6.3 displays the frequency distribution of fixations over the field on the Y axis with 7.6 cm regions defined around the center of the bar which coincided with the center of Region 14. During experimental periods 59% of all fixations were in Region 14 in contrast to 48% of all fixations during control periods.

ANOVAs run on the distribution of fixations along the Y axis produced no stable effects, with average Y variance almost exactly the same during experimental and control periods. However, as in Study 3, there was a striking increase in variance along the X axis (parallel) from control to experimental periods (6.53 cm and 11.73 cm, respectively; $F[1,12] = 9.7$, $p < .01$).

The fixation and distribution analyses of the present study, then, closely replicated those of Study 3 with edges. Subjects stayed nearer the bar

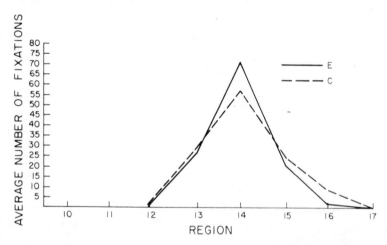

FIG. 6.3.   Frequency distribution of fixations across regions for experimental and control periods for horizontal bars in Study 4. (The regions each represent 7.62 cm height in the real field with the bar center lying in the center of Region 14.)

TABLE 6.1
Average Size of Eye Movement (cm) for Experimental
and Control Periods and for Each Movement Type for
Vertical Bars in Study 4

	Movement Type	
Period	Cross	No Cross
Experimental	4.22	2.08
Control	3.73	2.18

location, whether it was in a vertical or horizontal position, when it was actually there than when it was not.[2] Once again, the distribution of fixations was not reliably affected by either stimulus orientation except in the one, unexpected case, of an increase along the X (parallel) axis when the horizontal bar was presented.

Analyses of Eye Movements

Vertical Bar. As in Study 3, although eye movements were slightly larger during experimental than control conditions (2.74 vs. 2.62 cm), an analysis of size of eye movement revealed no stable effect of condition on the distance the eye moved, or on the size of movements along the X axis alone or the Y axis alone. The average distance moved was somewhat smaller than in Study 3— 2.54 cm and 2.82 cm for control and experimental periods as compared to 3.3 cm and 3.6 cm in the earlier study.

An analysis of percentage of movements which crossed either edge of the bar revealed a stable C effect, $F(1,12) = 19.7$, $p < .001$, with more crosses occurring during the experimental periods than the control periods (37% vs. 25% of all moves, respectively).

It will be remembered that one of the most interesting findings in Study 3 was a differentially 'large increase in the size of edge-cross eye movements during experimental periods. An analysis of size of eye movement as a function of bar-contour crossing was carried out for the present data. Table 6.1 displays the average size of eye movements as a function of period and whether or not they crossed one or more of the bar edges.

The ANOVA revealed that the T × C interaction was not stable, $F(1,12) = 2.93$, but as expected, the C factor was, $F(1,12) = 138.9$, $p < .001$. Although the statistical interaction was not stable, the pattern of means was

---

[2]It should be remembered that the center of the bar was placed at the predicted resting location of the eye during control periods, so it is not surprising that some of the experimental-control comparisons of average distance from center of the bar were only of marginal stability.

very similar to that of Table 5.3; that is, whereas no-cross scores were virtually identical for the two periods, cross scores for experimental periods were larger than for control. The increase was on the order of 13%, somewhat less than the 25% increase of the earlier study.

Horizontal Bar.   As for all other analyses in Studies 3 and 4 the size of eye movement was larger during experimental than control periods for the horizontal bar; however, for the first time, the effect was statistically stable with the average eye movement size larger for experimental than control periods (3.12 vs. 2.59 cm, respectively; $F(1,12) = 9.4$, $p < .01$). Separate analyses revealed that the increase in size of eye movements reflected primarily an increase in the size of the X-axis component, $F(1,12) = 10.7$, $p < .01$, although a marginally stable increment in the Y-axis component was also involved, $F(1,12) = 3.8$, $p < .10$. The increase in the X component of movement from control periods (1.70 cm) to experimental periods (2.18 cm) was substantial—on the order of 28%.

The percentage of eye movements that crossed the edge, as in Study 3, was greater for experimental (29%) than for control periods (24%), but the difference was not stable. The effects of the B variable on edge crosses found in the earlier study were not replicated here.

An analysis of size of eye movement as a function of type of movement was carried out for the horizontal bar data (see Table 6.2).

Analyses of variance revealed a stable T × C interaction, $F(1,12) = 5.6$, $p < .05$, and stable T and C effects. A B × T × C interaction ($p < .05$), probably attributable to chance, reflected a somewhat larger T × C interaction for the white-large screen condition than the black; both interactions were in the direction indicated by the table. Again, it will be noted that there was a relatively slight difference, .33 cm, between control and experimental periods for no-cross movements. The difference for cross movements was clearly more substantial—the percentage increase, this time, in the neighborhood of 21%.

TABLE 6.2
Average Size of Eye Movement (cm) for Experimental
and Control Periods and for Each Movement Type for
Horizontal Bars in Study 4

	Movement Type	
Period	Cross	No Cross
Experimental	4.50	2.67
Control	3.71	2.34

DISCUSSION

The replicability of findings in Study 3 by the findings of the present study was heartening indeed, as was the nonreplicability of such nuisance factors as Brightness and Sequence. An advantage of carrying out closely related studies in tandem is that one can obtain an indication of which nuisance factors can be ignored, as well as which important factors are worthy of discussion.

We can have strong confidence in several findings: the effect of both horizontal and vertical contours on average fixation location, the effect of horizontal contour on increasing X-axis variance, the tendency for newborns to cross contour when it is present, and the tendency for them to make larger eye movements when they cross a region that contains contours than when it does not. There was one finding that was unique to the present study; the strong increase in size of movement along the X axis, when a horizontal bar was presented, gives us more confidence in the marginal effect found in Study 3.

The unanticipated and exciting finding in both Studies 3 and 4 was the increase in size of edge-cross eye movements during experimental periods. The differences were not small, and the parameter estimated could be expected to be fairly stable since approximately 1900 eye movements were involved for each edge orientation and each bar orientation; for vertical crosses, the percentage increase in size of movement was 25% in the edge study and 13% for the bar. The corresponding percentage increase in size for horizontal crosses was 16% in the edge study and 21% for the bar.

The theoretical significance of this finding leans on facts known about adult eye movements. The determination of a future fixation is made before the eye moves and is not affected by stimulation which appears later than 40 msec preceding the initiation of the movement (Alpern, 1969; Fuchs, 1971; Komoda, Festinger, Phillips, Duckman, & Young, 1973; Stark, 1971). Also, the terminus of an eye movement is not affected by stimulation while the eye is in transit (Westheimer, 1954); in fact, the threshold for simple detection of a stimulus is drastically increased during eye movement (Volkmann, 1962; Volkmann, Schick, & Riggs, 1968). If these statements are true about the newborn eye-positioning system also, then it follows that the size of an edge-cross eye movement is not affected during the actual crossing of the edge, that is, while the eye is in flight; rather, the distance to be travelled is determined *before* the eye moves. By the evidence presented and the logic of this argument, the newborn "plans" to cross or process the edge before the movement is initiated. This finding is clearly contradictory to a "random-walk" notion of visual processing in newborns; that is, that edge contrasts exert their effect merely by attracting visual fixation. A more determined processing attack by the newborn is suggested. The increase in X-axis dispersion also suggests some attempt by the baby to adjust the scanning style to the stimulus so that crossing frequency is optimized.

The increase in dispersion of movements along the horizontal axis when a horizontal edge was presented was very substantial in both studies. Hebb (1949) speculated that even a line is not given in perception, that an infant must first trace the line to activate relevant cell assemblies for the organization of a perceptual line response.[3] Presumably, equal attraction tendencies would exist in peripheral or parafoveal vision to either side of a current fixation; visual fixations would thus be expected to trace the full line with some constraints. This interpretation helps to account for the increase in X variance for the horizontal edge. However, no effect was found on Y variance when the vertical edge was presented. Perhaps the infant eye is capable of only so many degrees of freedom along the vertical axis, and the full extent is used during control periods. If this is true, there are some interesting predictions deriving from Hebb's theory about the extent to which horizontal and vertical cell assemblies can be organized—possibilities that have interesting implications for early visual perception. The increase in fixation variance that was found for horizontal edges is especially remarkable, because either a significant *decrease* in X-axis scan variance during experimental periods has been reported (Salapatek, 1968; Salapatek & Kessen, 1966), or no change at all (Kessen et al., 1972). Stimulus-related changes along the Y axis have not been reported.

A second interpretation of the larger dispersion of fixations along the X axis for horizontal orientations, which neither supports nor refutes the Hebbian hypothesis, concerns more the eye movement than the dispersion of fixations. We have found repeatedly that the X component of an eye movement is virtually always larger than the Y component. In the present study, we found a significant increment in the size of the X component when a horizontal bar was presented, a tendency that was only marginally stable in Study 2 for the horizontal edge. As I argued in the discussion in Chapter 5, the newborn seems to move the eye on the axis that is easiest for the infant, namely the X axis, to accomplish what might seem easier by a perpendicular Y movement. Perhaps the baby makes larger X movements when an increase in the Y component of movement could be more efficient, because that is all the baby *can do* to cross the edge. This finding, then, is in line with an interpretation that places emphasis on edge crossing and consequent effects on cortical firing rate as factors that govern visual scanning and search. I elaborate on this idea in Chapter 9.

It is apparent that we must add a new rule to the newborn kitbag to accommodate the manner with which the infant deals with contour. The rule might read: "When you find an edge, scan near it and attempt to cross over it."

---

[3]I would like to thank Phillip Salapatek for his contribution to this discussion.

7

Study 5,
How Newborns Scan an Angle:
Do Angles Have Unique Effects?

The studies described in Chapters 3 through 6 employed very simple visual situations, the most complicated stimulus consisting of two linear and parallel black-white contours, a bar. Linear contours are not only uncomplicated geometrically, they are also simple neurophysiologically, detectable by simple cells in area 17 of the visual cortex, possibly at the level of the first cortical synapse. An interesting question is whether the newborn's visual behavior can be accounted for only in terms of contour-seeking and "contour-play" activity, or whether the newborn is responsive to higher-level pattern features. The answer to this question is important for deciding about what the necessary components of a comprehensive rule system are, as well as for theorizing about the level of brain organization at birth.

In a landmark study, Salapatek and Kessen (1966) showed newborns an equilateral, solid-black triangle on a white background and found that they constrained their fixations almost exclusively to a single angle, ignoring the linear sides. Angle attractiveness was again found by Salapatek (1968), but the linear sides were also found to be attractive; unfortunately, the interpretation of the attractiveness of sides was complicated by the fact that flashing infrared illuminators behind the sides of the triangle were slightly visible, which may have attracted the newborn's gaze. Regardless, it is widely believed that angles have a special attractive influence on the newborn (for example, Bond, 1972; Haber & Hershenson, 1973; see also Nelson & Kessen, 1969).

A conclusion often taken from the Salapatek and Kessen study is either that (1) angles are detected by the newborn but linear contour is not or (2) that angles are more attractive than linear contour. Angles might have higher priority because they are of greater "ecological importance," containing more stimulus information. Pursuing this same line of argument, the residual advantage that vertical contours had over horizontal contours in my studies (Studies 3 and 4)—for example, in the stability of the contour-crossing measure—could be attributed to the greater ecological import of vertical stimuli. Important, especially moving, events in the world are most frequently perpendicular to the horizon, a fact consistent with the lateral organization of the eyes and their natural tendency toward horizontal sweeps.

However, there were limitations of prior research that leave a more parsimonious and general interpretation tenable. Only 60° angles were used with newborns. Such angles are comprised of edges that lie very close together near the angle intercept. It could be the case, then, that the angle was preferred over the linear edges, not because it was an "angle," but because contour density was greater than along the linear sides. As the newborn scans an angle, two edges would be relocated near center retina, which would produce more firing than only the one edge found along the triangle sides. This interpretation is consistent with my earlier argument that the newborn stays near the portion of the visual field which, in combination with the newborn's natural scan tendencies, produces a high rate of cortical firing.

A second consideration guided the construction of the stimuli for this study. Studies 3 and 4 indicated that relocating the horizontal edges to an area that the newborn could easily scan strikingly reduced the differences with which the newborn scanned horizontal and vertical edges. However, the vertical contours still retained a higher degree of control over scanning by some measures—for example, in the number of edge crosses. One might still claim, in line with the ethological argument, that vertical contour is more attractive than horizontal. However, vertical contour has not yet been pitted against horizontal contour in the same stimulus. Here it was.

Stimuli were created that permitted direct comparison of the attractiveness of vertical and horizontal contours as well as the comparative attractiveness of these linear contours with that of a right angle. The vertical- and horizontal-bar stimuli of Study 4 were joined to connect, but not cross, which produced a vertical bar, a horizontal bar, an internal right angle, and an external right angle. Although it was difficult to say, a priori, what relative amounts of cortical stimulation would result from scanning each of these elements, the right angle was expected to produce less cortical firing than an acute angle. The reason for this expectation is illustrated in Fig. 7.1. Given that stimuli located near the fovea produce a relatively high rate of cortical firing because of high cell density and cortical magnification, the foveal region is highly important. As the illustration shows, an infant could fixate in more regions and keep two contours near the cell-rich fovea with an acute angle than with a right angle. An interesting question was whether the right angle would "bully" the bars in attracting fixations, as has been the case with acute angles. If so, special rules of scanning must be devised to accommodate

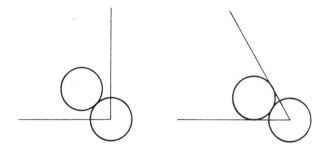

FIG. 7.1. Illustration of effect of fixating two points near an acute and a 90°
angle. A fixation at the intercept of either angle results in a foveal projection
(indicated by circle) of both angle sides. However, a fixation equidistant from
intercept and from sides results in a foveal projection of both sides only for the
acute angle.

newborns' responses to contour *organization*. If not, then no special
provision is required in a rule system to accommodate newborns' visual
activity to anything more complicated than local contour density.

METHOD

Subjects. Sixteen full-term, apparently normal, and awake newborn
infants (born at the Cambridge Hospital) between 24 and 96 hours of age
served as subjects in the present study. The data from several other infants
were not used because they fell asleep or cried ($n = 11$), moved too much or
did not photograph well ($n = 2$), because equipment malfunctioned ($n = 4$),
or for miscellaneous reasons (for example, experimenter error, $n = 6$).

Apparatus. The apparatus, room, noise level, and lighting were as
identical to that in Studies 3 and 4 as possible.

Stimuli. The 50.8 cm × 50.8 cm stimulus screens were prepared at the
same time and in exactly the same manner as those for the edge and bar
studies. Four screens were prepared which can be thought of as partial
combinations and deletions of the vertical and horizontal bar stimuli in the
bar study. On each stimulus a vertical and horizontal bar joined, but did not
intersect, thus forming an internal and an external angle. The four screens, as
shown in Fig. 7.2 were: (1) TVRH—the top portion of the vertical bar
combined with the right portion of the horizontal bar; (2) BVRH—the
bottom portion of the vertical bar combined with the right portion of the
horizontal bar; (3) TVLH—the top portion of the vertical bar combined with
the left portion of the horizontal bar; and (4) BVLH—the bottom portion of
the vertical bar combined with the left portion of the horizontal bar.

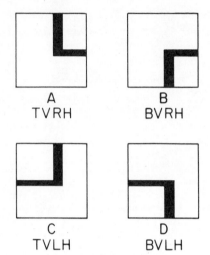

A
TVRH

B
BVRH

C
TVLH

D
BVLH

FIG. 7.2.   The stimulus screens used in Study 5.

The relevant dimensions of the stimuli were as follows (shown in Fig. 7.2 only for TVRH):

Vertical segment:	left side to left edge	26.3 cm
	right side to right edge	17.8 cm
Horizontal segment:	top to top edge	25.7 cm
	bottom to bottom edge	21.3 cm

The predicted resting location of the eye corresponded to a point halfway along an imaginary line that connected the internal and external angles. The bar components for all four screens were black and the fields white. A photometric reading of these stimuli yielded values of 7.37, 1.03, 2.57, and 2.81 cd/m^2 for the white, black, internal angle, and external angle regions, respectively. Control stimuli were homogeneous white scrrens.

Procedure.   All procedural details were as identical to those in the edge and bar studies as possible. Eight subjects were presented the TVLH and BVLH stimuli in sequence for 60 seconds (separated by the customary 30-second control period); the remaining eight were presented the TVRH and BVRH stimuli. Four subjects in each group saw the stimulus with the top element first; the other four saw the stimulus with the bottom element first.

RESULTS

The principal analysis for this study concerned the frequency with which newborns fixated in three areas: a square area containing the angle; a similar adjacent area containing part of the vertical bar; a similar adjacent area containing part of the horizontal bar. All areas attracted more fixations when the stimulus was actually presented. However, the angle was not differentially attractive. Considering only those fixations that fell within one of these three squares, the relative proportion of fixations that fell in the angle area actually declined from control to experimental periods.

Secondary analyses revealed that the large majority of infants scanned more than one region. Contour-region crossing was greater during experimental than during control periods. Because some areas did not attract a sufficient number of fixations during control periods, detailed control-experimental comparisons of parameters of eye movement were not possible in some cases. Additional details of analyses are given in the following.

Analyses of Eye Position and Distribution of Fixations. The attractiveness of the various components of the stimuli was first evaluated by drawing three 7.62 cm square regions: one around the center angles, one around the horizontal bar, and one around the vertical bar. The regions were, as mentioned, of equal size and were nonoverlapping but as close to visual center as possible. Thus extreme noncentral portions of the vertical and horizontal bars were excluded. Figure 7.3 displays the template used for scoring, with the regions for all four stimuli superimposed. Of course, only three regions were relevant for a particular stimulus. The number of fixations in each of the three relevant boxes was tallied for each stimulus for every subject.

The stimuli were strikingly attractive. There were more fixations in the three relevant boxes on experimental than control periods for 29 out of a total of 32 comparisons (two stimuli for each of 16 subjects). A breakdown of the number of subjects who increased or decreased their number of fixations in each of the regions is shown in Table 7.1. Top, bottom, right, and left regions were each relevant 16 times, whereas the center region was relevant for all 32 presentations. The percentage of occasions on which increases or decreases occurred is shown in parentheses. The table is easily summarized: In every region except the bottom, on 75% or more of the comparisons (excluding ties), more fixations were made during experimental than control trials. There was virtually no difference between control and experimental periods for the bottom region.

Although the data in Table 7.1 clearly suggest that all elements but the bottom element were attractive for the majority of subjects, it does not reflect what the relative strength of attractiveness of these elements was. The top portion of Table 7.2 gives the average number of fixations made in each relevant region for the two presentations of each stimulus. Table 7.3 gives the *distributional* percentage for each box—that is, the percentage of all fixations falling within each box of the total number falling in any one of the relevant boxes. This breakdown addresses the question: For only the fixations in the relevant areas, what proportion fell in each region?

The data were remarkably stable either when represented in terms of average number of fixations in various regions or in distributional per-

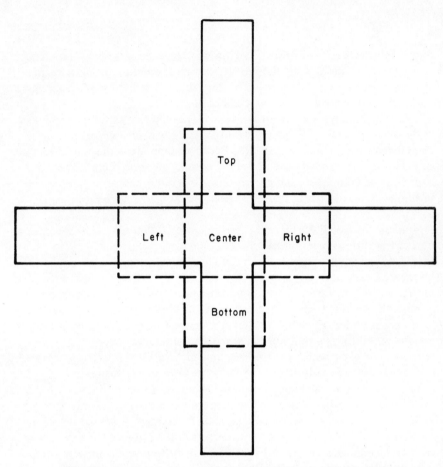

FIG. 7.3. Prototype used to define regions for calculation of fixation distributions in angle study. For all stimuli, the Center Region was relevant, but for any one stimulus, only one vertically adjacent and one horizontally adjacent region were relevant.

TABLE 7.1
Number of Subjects Showing an Increase, Decrease, or Equal
Fixations from Control to Experimental Periods in Various Regions
of the Stimulus in Study 5

Region	Direction of Change from Control to Experimental Periods					
	Increase		Decrease		Tie	
Top	8	(50%)	2	(12.5)	6	(37.5)
Right	12	(75)	4	(25)	-	
Bottom	7	(43.8)	6	(37.5)	3	(18.7)
Left	12	(75)	4	(25)	-	
Center	24	(75)	8	(25)	-	

Note. Percentage of occasions shown in parentheses.

TABLE 7.2

Average Number of Fixations in Each Region of the Stimuli for Control and Experimental Periods in Study 5

| | Region | | | | | | | | | | | |
| | Top | | Right | | Center | | Bottom | | Left | | Total | |
Stimulus	Con	Exp	Con	Exp	Con	Exp	Con	Exp	Con	Exp	Con	Exp
⌐	5.4	6.9			32.1	40.6			4.1	32.9	41.6	80.4
⌐	4.9	8.1	17.6	28.5	29.4	52.0					51.9	88.6
Γ					33.0	44.2	5.1	4.8	5.0	36.5	43.1	85.5
L			12.4	24.0	30.2	59.2	4.4	13.2			47.0	96.4

TABLE 7.3

Proportional Distribution of Fixations That Fell in the Relevant Regions for Control and Experimental Periods in Study 5

| | Region | | | | | | | | | |
| | Top | | Right | | Center | | Bottom | | Left | |
Stimulus	Con	Exp	Con	Exp	Con	Exp	Con	Exp	Con	Exp
⌐	13.0%	8.6%			77.0%	50.5%			10.0%	40.9%
⌐	9.4%	9.1%	33.9%	32.3%	56.6%	58.7%				
Γ					76.6%	51.7%	11.8%	5.6%	11.6%	42.7%
L			26.4%	24.9%	64.3%	61.0%	9.4%	13.7%		

83

centages. During control periods, when no stimulus was presented, the center-box area was most popular, containing an average of from 29.4 to 33 fixations for the four stimuli, 56.6% to 77% of all fixations falling in one of the relevant areas. In experimental periods the average number of fixations in the central region increased to between 40.6 and 59.2, but the *percentage* of all relevant fixations in that region *decreased* for every orientation but one. The percentages during experimental periods ranged from 50.5% to 61%. The one increase was slight indeed, whereas the percentage decrease for two of the stimuli was substantial. Top and bottom elements contained close to only 10% of fixations during control periods, and, in three of four cases, this percentage *decreased* during experimental trials. The right element contained between 26% and 34% of the fixations during control periods, and these percentages remained almost constant during experimental periods. The only striking increase in distributional percentages occurred for the left-horizontal element in both cases—from 10% and 11.6% during control periods to 40.9% and 42.7% during experimental periods. Thus, in terms of the distribution of fixations, there was little change from control to experimental periods except that the center, angle, region actually lost distributional favor whereas the left, horizontal, region gained favor.

It it interesting to note the substantially greater attractiveness of horizontal over vertical elements in this study due, probably, to the location of the vertical elements above and below an easy range of viewing and crossing by the infant.

One additional measure was taken to inquire about whether or not subjects were responding on a part- or whole-form basis. A calculation was made of how many subjects made 10 or more fixations in at least two of the three relevant boxes; 25 of 32 subjects did so suggesting that there was at least some exploration of more than one component.

To further examine fixation data, analyses of variance were carried out on the average X and Y position in the field and on the variance in distribution of X and Y fixations. The analyses contained two between-subject variables—Side (S, horizontal bar to the right or left) and Order (O, up-bar or down-bar stimulus presented first)—and two within-subject variables—Height (H, vertical bar up or down) and Condition (C, experimental vs. control).

An analysis of position along the X axis revealed a stable C effect with average fixation nearer to field center during experimental than control periods, 3.30 cm vs. 10.54 cm to the right of center, $F(1,12) = 17.6, p < .001$, and a S × C and O × C interaction (both $p < .05$). Table 7.4 displays the means comprising the S × C interaction that reflects, primarily, the greater positioning of the eye to the right during experimental periods when the right bar was presented than when the left bar was presented.

The O × C interaction was uninteresting, reflecting primarily a substantially larger right-going tendency during control periods in the UP-DOWN order than the DOWN-UP order, 13.87 cm vs. 7.21 cm to the right.

TABLE 7.4

Average Deviation (from Center of Field) of Fixation
Along the X Axis During Control and Experimental
Periods When the Horizontal Segment Was on the Left
or the Right Side in Study 5

Side	Period	
	Control	Experimental
Right	9.98 cm	6.58 cm
Left	11.10 cm	0.00

Note. Positive scores indicate distance to the right of field
center.

An analysis of eye position along the Y axis revealed only a S × C
interaction ($p < .05$), this time reflecting what would appear to be a chance
difference in the two side groups during control periods. These data are
shown in Table 7.5. Despite the differences in control-period orientation,
both groups were drawn closer to the horizontal bar position of –2.54 cm
during experimental conditions.

An ANOVA on variance along the X axis and variance along the Y axis
produced no results of theoretical interest.

Analyses of Eye Movements.   Analyses using the same independent
variables as described in the previous discussion were carried out on eye-
movement data also. There were no stable effects of experimental variables
on the total size of eye movements or on the size of the X or Y components.
The average size of the movements was 3.3 cm for both experimental and
control periods, quite close to the values found for Studies 3 and 4.

An analysis of the number of times subjects crossed one or more contour
boundaries was carried out. Subjects averaged more contour location crosses

TABLE 7.5

Average Deviation (from Center of Field) of Fixation
Along the Y Axis During Control and Experimental
Periods When the Horizontal Segment Was on the Left
or the Right Side in Study 5

Side	Period	
	Control	Experimental
Right	–2.01 cm	–2.82 cm
Left	–3.51 cm	–2.41cm

Note. Negative scores indicate distance below field center.

TABLE 7.6
Average Size of Eye Movements for the Horizontal
Segment on the Right Side as a Function of Whether
the Contour Position Was Crossed or Not

	Type of Movement	
Period	Cross	No Cross
Experimental	3.07 cm	2.16 cm
Control	2.74 cm	2.29 cm

during experimental than control trials (34.4 vs. 18.8; $F(1,12) = 31.8$, $p < .001$). An analysis of number of times a horizontal contour location was crossed revealed similar findings (24.7 vs. 10.8; $F(1,12) = 24.6, p < .001$), but there was not a stable effect for vertical contour-location crosses (13.3 vs. 10.0; $F(1,12) = 1.41, p < .25$).

Some difficulty was encountered in attempting to carry out an analysis on size of eye movements as a function of whether or not the edge was crossed. There were not a sufficient number of vertical bar crosses to include those data and, when only horizontal crosses were considered, it was found that six of eight babies in the LVDH condition had no crosses during control periods. Therefore, an analysis was carried out only on the babies presented a bar segment on the right side, and then, only for horizontal crosses. As expected, the Type factor (cross vs. no cross) was stable, $F(1,12) = 16.9$, $p < .01$, reflecting larger movements for cross than for no-cross movements. Not surprising because of such few observations, this analysis did not yield a stable Period X Type interaction ($F(1,12) = 2.19$, $p < .10$). However, it is interesting that the same direction of results was obtained for this study as for Studies 3 and 4 (see Table 7.6). Whereas there was little difference (.13 cm) between control and experimental trials when the eye did not cross a contour location, there was a difference when it did cross; the increase in size of eye movement was about 12%, somewhat smaller than that found in Studies 3 and 4.

This is the fifth independent analysis that has revealed the same relation indicating larger eye movements when newborns cross a region, and the contour is actually there, than when they cross the identical region but the contour is absent.

DISCUSSION

This study provided interesting information on several questions about newborn visual scanning. The stimuli used were remarkably compelling for newborns; even when fixations only on the centrally located portions of the horizontal and vertical segments were considered as "on stimulus," between

67% and 80% of all experimental time was spent by newborns in one of the three relevant regions. These areas contained only 35% to 43% of the fixations during control periods. Thus, we may assume that these stimuli actively engaged the newborn's processing activity.

A central question asked in this study was whether or not the angle would "bully" the vertical and horizontal segments of the stimuli. It did not. Although the absolute number of fixations in the angle region did increase from control to experimental trials for all stimuli, the absolute number of fixations increased for every other region also, with but one exception for only one stimulus. When one asks, however, how the distribution of fixations in the relevant regions was affected by presentation of the stimuli, a different picture emerges.

The percentage of fixations in the central region actually dropped from control to experimental periods for three stimuli and increased by ony 2% in the fourth. During control trials, an average of approximately 69% of fixations in relevant regions were in the angle region, whereas during experimental periods, this figure dropped to about 56%. For segments in the top, bottom, and right regions, the distributional percentages remained fairly constant from control to experimental periods (top, 11% to 9%; right, 30% to 29%; bottom, 11% to 9% for control and experimental periods, respectively). Only the left region showed a substantial increment in distributional percentage, shifting from an average of 11% during control periods to 42% during experimental periods. The unusually low percentage during the control periods was somewhat of a surprise, but the large increment during the experimental period did demonstrate, at the least, that the angle did not differentially attract fixations when it was present and that horizontal elements can powerfully influence looking behavior. The most important thing to be taken from the distributional finding is that angles are not universally overwhelming for the newborn and that the hypothesis of "stimulation potential" rather than angularity or "form" is tenable to account for newborn scanning of form.

A secondary question in this study was what would happen when vertically oriented elements were pitted against horizontally oriented elements. The outcome helped to clear up some aspects of our earlier findings. Table 7.3 shows that the increase in absolute number of fixations for the horizontal segments was much greater than for the vertical segments. The average increment from control to experimental periods gives the same picture, although the left element was responsible for most of the horizontal-segment increase.

The interesting aspect of this finding is that it is a clear reversal of the Kessen et al. study and a shift from the negative results of the bar and edge studies that suggest no striking horizontal-vertical differences. The critical factor appears to be the placement of the stimuli relative to the baby's visual center. Although top, bottom, and left regions controlled almost exactly the same average number of fixations during the control period (an average of 5.2, 4.8, and 5.6 fixations, respectively), the top and bottom regions still attracted very few fixations when vertical segments were actually presented during experimental periods (an average of 7.5 and 9 fixations, respectively), whereas the left segment produced a striking increase (an average of 34.7 fixations). Clearly, this finding suggests that the Kessen et al. results did reflect less advantageous placement of horizontal bars for newborns than for vertical bars. Here we have shown that vertical bars may be placed so that they are virtually ignored also. But the problem is not simply one of detection; newborns go into the regions containing all segments but they do not stay in those regions when they are outside of a band about ±9⁰ above and below visual center. It seems likely that they do not stay in those regions because the elements can not be easily crossed.

In addition to what this finding may suggest regarding the factors that control newborn scanning, there is an important methodological point. Investigators have not concerned themselves with the role that the placement of visual elements in a stimulus might play for newborns and young infants. The impact of a stimulus has generally been considered to be definable strictly in physical terms with no concern whatever for the babies ability to act on it. I would guess that, outside a ±9° band on the Y axis, stimuli are virtually ignored by the newborn. The center of this band lies at the natural resting position of the newborn's eye, which is, in turn, affected by head positioning. And although we may reasonably assume this "band" expands with age, it is not clear at what rate. Consider a familiar control stimulus in studies of attractiveness of face configurations to make the point. Frequently the face is simply inverted, and the assumption made that all elements are still "available" to the infant. But it could be that the relative potency of certain critical features, such as the eyes, may fall outside the "band of stimulus potency" for one of the orientations. In short, the baby may, in responding differently to upright and inverted faces, be responding to presence of eyes in the baby's "band of stimulus potency" in one case and absence of eyes in that band in the other, rather than to any more abstract "gestalt" factors.

The fact that newborns entered more than one region with substantial frequency suggests that they are not limited, necessarily, to single-element processing as suggested by Salapatek and Kessen. This is a problem that needs further study, but it does seem reasonable that whether the newborn is characterized as a part- or whole-form processor will depend, as Salapatek (1968) has suggested, on the stimulus and how regions are defined. Salapatek and Kessen's early finding of single-angle processing by newborns may have reflected, in part, the high density of contour at the angle that reduced scan variance and, hence, suggested that the newborn was a single-element processor. However, as I found in the edge and bar studies, a stimulus with a low density of contours may produce relatively broad scan variance, resulting in a high probability of multiregion entry.

8

Summation of Findings and Elaboration of the Rule System

This chapter is organized into three sections. The first section is a summary of conclusions of the five studies. Section two succinctly organizes what we now know about newborn visual activity and presents the rules required to account for newborn behavior. Section three relates earlier work to the proposed rule system.

SUMMARY OF CONCLUSIONS

Study 1. Study 1 compared visual scanning of newborns in complete darkness and in unpatterned light. Babies scanned actively in darkness in a well-controlled and detailed manner. The eyelids were frequently open to the point of strain, suggesting a degree of tenseness and extreme alertness. On the other hand, newborns scanned lit, unpatterned fields broadly with larger eye movements; eye control was frequently lost as the eyes engaged in nystagmus near the lateral or nasal canthi. Whereas the more detailed scanning in darkness seems appropriate for discovery of shadows, subtle edges, or small spots, the broader scanning in light seems suited to discovery of bold contours.

The major conclusion from these findings is that newborns are congenitally equipped to engage in visual activity that maximizes the likelihood that they will find available visual information. This "seek" operation is endogenously controlled, that is, not dependent on external stimulation for its activation or maintenance. A second conclusion is that a qualitative difference in visual activity exists between light and dark scanning; different control systems appear to be engaged under these two conditions. The possibility that the difference merely reflected a continuum of responsiveness to light intensity was deemed unlikely inasmuch as a large difference in field brightness in the two light conditions had virtually no effect on any of the parameters studied. I suggested that scanning in light is organized, at least partially, around visual inputs; when those inputs are unavailable, as in the case of a homogeneous field, the baby often loses eye control.

Study 2.   The effects of rate of light onset and offset on alert and asleep newborns were examined in Study 2. The major results of Study 1 were replicated giving me strong confidence in these findings. (I should add that the dark findings reported here have also been replicated in three additional studies reported on by Mendelson and Haith, 1976.) Given the variability of newborn data and the number of empirical contradictions that characterize this field, replication is no mean feat. Although definitive data were not obtained on whether sudden light offset could produce a response from newborns even in deep sleep, results did help clarify whether differences in light and dark scanning are qualitative or quantitative. Once again eye opening to the point of strain occurred more frequently in darkness than in light, and once again it is reasonable to ask if the brightness of the light in the light condition simply inhibited extreme opening. However, this more parsimonious interpretation was further weakened by the finding that eyelid opening to abrupt light onset was greater than to gradual light onset; because of dark adaptation we would expect just the opposite if the screen were bright enough to suppress lid opening.

While helping to cast doubt on one quantitative interpretation of light-dark differences in visual activity, the greater eye opening after abrupt transitions raised the possibility that degree of eyelid opening simply reflects arousal level, with rapid change producing more arousal than gradual change. Carried one step further, greater eye opening in darkness may simply mean that darkness is more arousing than light; so, in reality, the light-dark differences we saw may have reflected a quantitative difference. But "arousal level" cannot be the whole story either, because some of the effects of abrupt light onset were different from those of dark. Abrupt light onset produced more out-of-control nystagmus and fewer smooth movements than gradual onset. The opposite relation held for these variables in darkness and light. Thus, the pool of dependent variables did not hang together in a manner that suggests that darkness and abrupt onset affect scanning through a common arousal mechanism.

Study 3.   Through Study 3 we examined the newborn's scanning of the simplest visual patterns—a horizontal and a vertical edge. In some respects, Study 3 replicated earlier findings of a similar study by Kessen et al. (1972). Linear edges were compelling for the newborn, attracting the baby's gaze and engaging contour-crossing activity. But in contrast to that study in which edges were placed about 18⁰ away from the center of the field, here the centered horizontal edge affected scanning as much as the vertical edge. Given that even vertical edges lose their appeal when placed above or below 9⁰ of the center of the field (Study 5), it seems clear that stimuli are effective for the newborn only within a narrow horizontal band. I concluded that stimuli outside this band are not as attractive because edge crossing is not easily accomplished. This interpretation fits the more general hypothesis that the attractiveness of a contour is related to how easily it may be crossed or relocated on the retina near the foveal region. An important conclusion is that stimuli for the newborn are not inherently attractive or unattractive; they "occupy" the newborn to the extent that the baby's action on them produces a favorable result. Or, stated differently, it is the consequences of the sensorimotor loop that control visual scanning, so both the properties of the stimulus, and the newborn's oculomotor skills must be considered.

Study 3 did reveal an interesting difference in the response of the infant to horizontal and vertical edges. For the first time, I found that newborns increased their breadth of scanning to a visual pattern. In line with earlier studies, newborns scanned slightly more narrowly when the vertical edge was presented. However, in contrast to earlier studies, scan variance increased by 93% when the horizontal edge was presented. One explanation of this increase is that fixations along the horizontal axis have only minor limiting constraints and that a vertical contour is needed as an anchor point to prevent drift. However, in blank-field control trials, an anchor point was also unavailable, and scan variance was 93% less. More likely, the increase in scanning variance along the horizontal axis (for horizontal edges) reflected the newborn's attempts to cross the edge. Since vertical movement is so difficult, these attempts manifested themselves primarily in more extensive fixations along the horizontal axis. (Other examples exist of babies doing what they do easiest rather than what is most efficient; for example, older babies move mouths and trunk in the initial stages of trying to reach for objects [Bruner, 1968].) Tendencies in the eye-movement data support this idea. The size of eye movements increased in the presence of the horizontal edge, and the X-axis component of these movements was primarily responsible for this increase; the vertical component also increased, but only slightly. The frequency of horizontal-bar crossing also increased.[1]

---

[1]These "tendencies" were of marginal reliability. However, several of the so-called "marginal" findings would have reached acceptable levels of statistical reliability had I simply included vertical and horizontal edge data in the same analysis. Thus, the increase in vertical-edge crossing was quite stable ($p < .001$) whereas that for horizontal-edge crossing was marginal. Size of eye movements increased for both the horizontal and vertical edges, more so for the horizontal-movement than for the vertical-movement component, but in most cases these individual analyses revealed only strong trends. I feel that the gain in statistical stability by combined analyses would have been offset by a loss in communicability of the findings as well as less appreciation of the repeatability of the findings.

The notion that a newborn "attempts" to cross a contour (relocate it on the retina near the foveal region) is rather radical in that it implies at least the rudiments of goal orientation for an organism that is commonly held to be subcortical and reflexive. A more parsimonious interpretation of contour-crossing activity is simply that the newborn has a tropism for high-contrast edges. Given this constraint of the average fixation location, a random walk would produce more edge crossing during experimental than control periods. This argument does not account, by itself, for larger eye movements and wider horizontal expanse (over horizontally orientated stimuli) during stimulus periods, nor does it account for the differentially large increase in size of eye movements that cross an edge. But, rather than propose that the "decorticate" newborn is capable of even a minimal amount of goal-oriented behavior, why not entertain the notion that as a light excites a moth contour-contrast "excites" (increases the activation level) the newborn? Such excitement would simply be reflected in larger eye movements and wider fixation distribution, much as one finds frenetic flying and covering of a wider area when that flying nemesis discovers a light. A weak contradiction to this characterization is that whereas vertical edges elicited larger eye movements and a more constrained fixation distribution along the horizontal axis, horizontal edges produced larger eye movements but an expanded range of fixation. Thus, at the least, the newborn selectively modifies behavior which puts the infant at least one up on the moth.[2]

The more compelling counterargument leans on the cross/no-cross analysis for experimental and control periods. The size of eye movements that crossed the contour area were 25% larger when the vertical edge was there than when it was not and 16% larger when the horizontal edge was presented. This increase was not simply a function of greater "excitement" during experimental periods; eye movements that did not cross the contour area were virtually identical in size during control and experimental periods. Since the terminus of an eye movement is determined before the eye moves, stimuli striking the fovea during flight cannot change the size of the movement. If the size of the eye movement that crossed the edge region was larger when the edge was actually there than when it was not, newborns must have selectively programmed the larger edge-cross movement. With this argument, we may reject the random-walk hypothesis or even the contour-elicited excitement hypothesis.

The important conclusions from Study 3, then, are that (1) newborns respond to edges that are vertically or horizontally oriented through

---

[2]This analogy was not chosen accidentally. It is fairly broadly assumed that the newborn is a decorticate animal who possesses nothing more than automatic reflexes. Although it is well known that the newborn will turn toward a light, it is also generally assumed that this behavior reflects nothing more than a tropism akin to behaviors observed in the lowest light-sensitive organisms.

relocating the "center-of-gravity" of their scan routine and by crossing them; (2) edge crossing is "planful" and not simply a by-product of greater proximity to the edge area or of generalized excitement during experimental periods; (3) the newborn appears to have a relatively small horizontal band in the visual field in which stimuli are effective. (This is probably the case because the newborn has difficulty making perpendicular eye movements along the vertical axis away from visual center. This difficulty probably increases with increasing distance of the starting point from center.)

Study 4. In Study 4 we examined the newborn's scanning of vertical and horizontal bars. These bars were designed to vary in width to equate their crossability on the basis of expected variance in fixation along the axis perpendicular to their orientation. By equating crossability of edges in Study 4, I hoped to clarify the finding of greater attractiveness of vertical over horizontal edges obtained in the Kessen et al. study and expected from Study 3 in this series. However, the data from Study 3 revealed that both horizontal and vertical edges were attractive, which can be interpreted to mean that crossability depends, to a large extent, on the location of stimuli in the field. Thus, the attempt to equate crossability by presenting multiple edges whose distance was based on scan variance was unnecessary.

However, Study 4 was notable for the consistent replication of findings from Study 3, including those that were a surprise and that are crucial to some of my arguments. The expected findings that replicated were closer proximity of fixations to the bar area in experimental as opposed to control periods for horizontal as well as vertical orientations and more crossing of the edge locations during experimental periods.

The surprising finding in Study 3 of an increase of 93% in the variance of fixation along the horizontal axis when a horizontal edge was presented was replicated in this study with an increase of 80% when a horizontal bar was presented. Further replication included a slight decrement in fixation variance for the vertical bar and a reliable increase in size of eye movement when horizontal bars were presented.

The important finding in Study 3 of a larger difference in size of eye movement for edge-cross movements than for no-cross movements was replicated in this study for both the vertical and horizontal bars. The size of the difference was somewhat smaller than in the previous study—13% for the vertical bar and 21% for the horizontal bar.

Study 5. In Study 5 I compared the relative attractiveness, within the same stimulus, of vertical and horizontal bars and an angle. The stimulus configurations were very compelling. Boxes, 7.6 cm square, drawn around the areas containing the angle and the center-most portions of the vertical and the horizontal bars, were found to contain an average of 73% of all fixations when the stimulus was presented as opposed to 38% when it was not. Given the rather diffuse scan of which a newborn is capable and that there were other, noncentral, bar portions of the stimuli to look at, this difference was substantial.

The presence of the stimulus during experimental periods increased fixations more for horizontal components than for vertical components; in fact, the vertical components enjoyed the smallest absolute increase of all. In conjunction with the findings of Kessen et al., that horizontal edges 18⁰ off center do not attract fixations, these results strengthen the claim that any stimuli placed outside a relatively narrow band in the newborn's visual field will not substantially affect looking behavior.

The distributional analysis suggested there is nothing special about angles for the newborn. The left horizontal stimulus component was the only one to increase in distributional percentage from control to experimental periods (31%). The percentages for the right, top, and bottom areas decreased very slightly, all less than 2.5%, whereas the central-angle area decreased more than 13%.

The analysis of size of eye movement as a function of whether or not an edge was crossed once again revealed that edge-cross movements were larger than control movements traversing the same area. This result was not significant, but only a limited amount of data could be used. However, this was the fifth analysis in which this relation held with no reversals. The difference was on the order of 12% for experimental periods and 6% in the reverse direction for control periods—reasonably similar to values obtained in the other studies. Hence, I feel great confidence may be placed in this finding.

The most important conclusions from Study 5 are (1) newborns may not respond to formal characteristics of stimuli more complicated than edges or edge density, (in contradiction to an angle-selection tendency as suggested by Salapatek and Kessen); (2) newborns respond to stimuli only within a narrow horizontal band in their visual field.

A RULE SYSTEM FOR NEWBORN SCANNING

With these findings before us in summary form, what can we say about the capabilities and inclinations the newborn possesses for acquiring information about the visual world? I have found it useful to assume that newborn scanning is governed by a limited set of rules that determine visual activity in fairly simple visual circumstances. These "rules" facilitate contact with important aspects of the environment. Of course, I assume that certain perceptual capabilities are available to the newborn, such as sensitivity to light, pattern, movement, perhaps color. But I feel that physical dimensions have been overemphasized in newborn research and the self-initiated, information-seeking skills de-emphasized, with the result that the newborn has been characterized as a multidimensional filter, at best, a multiple-choice selector of what stimulus to process. From my perspective, it is less important what a newborn can perceive than how the infant is organized to acquire visual information.

It seems strange to me that so much emphasis has been placed on stimulus controls over young-infant behavior and so little on the infant's own organization for acquiring visual information. This is so for two reasons. First, what "knowledge" a living system possesses must be less important than the tools that system possesses for gaining knowledge. Obviously these tools determine throughout life how an indefinite amount of information relevant to the culture and society will be acquired. If biology were to standardize anything, one would suspect that optimal strategies for acquiring information would have a very high priority. For some reason however, illustrated well by the intelligence-testing tradition, psychologists have traditionally focused on content as opposed to function.

The second reason is that whereas it is difficult to imagine a single dimension of visual input that would serve an infant well across the diverse conditions of human existence, it is not difficult to imagine universal acquisition strategies that would lead to useful information, independent of the specific condition. Thus, one might suspect that search activity is congenitally organized and that the shaping of perceptual analyzers awaits particular experiences that this activity produces. This latter formulation makes a great deal more sense to me, and I think it makes more adaptive sense also. Mendelson and Haith (1976) have made a similar argument with respect to the baby's structuring of amodal space. I pursue the matter further in the next chapter.

Given that some organization does exist at birth, we can ask how it is best described. In the studies reported in the earlier chapters I adopted the approach of giving the baby the maximum degree of freedom in visual search keeping the stimulus situations simple. In this way the natural organization of activity could emerge. From my point of view, the organization can best be described in terms of rules the baby appears to obey and the baby's tasks under different sets of visual circumstances.

Gould (1976) summarized a number of findings from the eye-movement literature on scanning of pictures. His summary, if accepted, leads to an interesting inference: "eye fixations are influenced by physical parameters, such as color and geometric features of the picture, the task requirements, the relationships of the objects in the pictures, and the viewer's intentions and strategies [p. 331]."

The "task" can not be manipulated for a newborn, and I believe that most would argue that the terms "intentions" and "strategies" do not apply at this age. However, I believe we can think of biology as setting the "task" and the equivalent of "intentions" and "strategies." If so, biologically fixed "tasks," "intentions," and "strategies" might be discoverable by careful analysis of eye-movement patterns. I consider the "rules" described in the following to be the equivalent of intentions and strategies in Gould's description for the newborn. And I believe the "task" also to be set by biology: to keep visual cortical firing rate at a high level (more on this task in the following discussion). Let us take a look at the rules I have found.

These rules proceed roughly from the most simple and general visual settings to more complex and specific settings:

Rule 1. If awake and alert and light not too bright, open eyes (support: Studies 1-5).

Rule 2. If in darkness, maintain a controlled, detailed search (support: Studies 1 and 2). *Comment:* This endogenously controlled search in darkness probably maximimizes detection of subtle shadows or edges, although it may also serve to increase the probability of finding limited lit areas.

Rule 3. If in light with no form, search for edges by relatively broad, jerky sweeps of the field (support: Studies 1 and 2). *Comment:* This type of search seems best suited for detection of bold contours. The presence of light appears to inhibit or suppress the endogenous control system so that exogenous stimuli may gain control. Consequently, in unpatterned light the newborn frequently loses eye control.

Rule 4. If an edge is found, terminate the broad scan and stay in the general vicinity of that edge. Attempt to implement eye movements that cross the edge. If such eye movements are not possible in the region of the edge (as is the case for edges too distant from the center of the field), scan for other edges (support: Studies 3-5). *Comment:* Scanning in the presence of contours reflects neurological and muscular constraints; thus, what a baby can do with an edge affects how compelling it will be.

Rule 5. While in the proximity of edges, reduce the disperson of fixations perpendicular to the edges as local and resolvable contour-density increases. (support: Acute angles, as in the Salapatek and Kessen study, reduced fixation variance as did the stimuli in Studies 3-5 on the perpendicular axis.) *Comment:* This rule, although not enjoying strong current support, makes it possible to explain several findings in the literature and to predict what newborns will do with more complex stimuli. However, the tentativeness of this rule is acknowledged.

What can we say is *not* true of newborn visual behavior?

1. Newborns possess only visual reflexes to available light stimuli, such as tropisms toward light and tracking of moving objects; more complicated visual behavior develops later from these reflexes (refutation: dark-scanning behaviors in Studies 1 and 2).

2. Newborn visual behavior is almost uniformly uncontrolled (refutation: dark-scanning behavior in Studies 1 and 2 and by contour scanning in Studies 3–5).

3. Newborns may be attracted to light or contrast, but their scanning behavior consists essentially of a random walk (refutation: changes in scan variance to contours in Studies 3–5, but most importantly, by evidence that eye movements that crossed contour areas differed when stimuli were present and absent).

4. Newborns are incapable of any semblance of goal-oriented activity (refutation: same data as for number 3).

5. Newborn-scanning behavior is not adaptable (refutation: results from virtually every study of scanning behavior).

6. Newborns are "attuned" to some configurations or orientations of visual stimuli over others (refutation: scanning of at least our stimuli, especially in Study 5). *Comment:* This refutation does not have strong support. Obviously, not all configurations have been tried.

7. Newborns are "captured" by stimuli rather than capturing them (refutation: data from Studies 3–5 and all studies of newborn scanning that have been conducted). *Comment:* Newborns find highly contoured forms in their visual field to be very compelling in terms of the amount of time they spend looking at them. However, they also engage in an active detailed scan over these stimuli almost always moving their eyes at least every half-second. Thus, they hardly seem "captured" by the stimuli in the sense of a hypnotic or trance-like compulsion to look at them.

OBSERVATIONS AND EARLIER WORK
RELEVANT TO THE RULE SYSTEM

The rules proposed in the preceding section grew out of the studies reported earlier in the book; however, they make sense with regard to earlier research, and they also have implications for early activity that extend well beyond the laboratory.

Visual Activity in Darkness. Rule 1 specified that alert, awake babies will open their eyes in light that is not too bright. Although I have not done a full-scale examination of the effects of intensity level on degree of eye opening, the light-dark differences we found when even dim light was used were striking. In Study 2, the "tracking" of the gradual transition in light intensity by lid opening was quite obvious. This rule has obvious methodological implications for work involving monitoring or control of the newborn state. Every newborn-state scale of which I am aware uses eye opening as an indication of alertness. Yet, hardly any mention is made of ambient illumination during the test or experiment. I am not saying that newborns will never open their eyes in a bright room; casual observation of visual behavior of newborns in the brightly lit nurseries of hospitals suggests otherwise. However, it is also clear that moderately bright light, as defined for an adult, does have an inhibitory effect on visual activity in newborns. As mentioned in Chapter 1, the ambient light level also affects the newborn's response to auditory stimuli (Kearsley, 1973).

An interesting possibility suggested by many subjective observations and by our difficulty in obtaining asleep babies in Study 2, is that dark conditions may actually wake babies up, or, depending on the perspective, light makes them sleep. Some data from the Iowa Child Welfare Station in the 1930s are suggestive. Studies by Weiss (1933, 1934) and by Irwin and Weiss (1934) demonstrated greater activity of newborns in darkness than in light and an inverse relation between various light levels and activity.

Several studies suggest that sleep occurs not through a fatiguing of nerve centers but rather through active suppression by one center of others. A. H. Parmelee (personal communication) suggested that the newborn may need sensory input to keep the suppressor system active. Darkness, constituting a situation of sensory deprivation, might not provide the suppressor system with sufficient stimulation to keep it active, resulting in awakening. This interpretation fits with the well-known phenomenon of diurnal-cycle reversals experienced by new parents in their babies: newborn babies often sleep during the day and scream at night. Brackbill, Adams, Crowell, and Gray (1966) found more activity of newborns in darkness and, in partial support of Salk (1960, 1961, 1962), that repetitive sounds quiet the newborn. By personal observation and casual report I have learned that the obvious solution of turning on a light in the baby's room at night can help a young infant sleep, but I know of no careful research on this issue. Perhaps the fact that nurseries are typically kept well-lit is no accident; overworked nursery-staff nurses may find their task facilitated when their charges sleep most of the time.

Piaget's (1951) theory of development stresses more than do most the role of the active organism in the creation of the organism's perceptual world. Yet, Piaget has little to say about the newborn and the baby's early perceptual acquisitions except to endow the newborn with a traditional set of reflexes to exogenous stimulation. Rule 2 suggests that the "starting point" does not depend on sensory competence alone or in stereotyped reflexes to sensory input; rather, the starting point is a congenitally organized information-acquisition routine. Major theorists of developmental perception such as Hebb, Gibson, and Piaget have either ignored or had great difficulty in getting the newborn going, so that the principles of perceptual development they suggest could take hold. Starting points have posed problems in almost all theories of development because virtually all address themselves to how additons or changes are made in already available structures. I might add that the dialogue concerning newborn competence has usually focused on what structures exist, but hardly ever have theorists concerned themselves with what *functions* exist in the newborn for acquiring knowledge.

The well-controlled visual scan in darkness is intriguing. If ever the newborn were to manifest difficulties in visual control, one would expect such difficulty to be most obvious in a situation of complete absence of visual stimuli. Yet, in this situation the newborn displays well-controlled, smooth search behavior. Roffwarg et al. (1966), studying REM sleep changes with age, found that newborns manifested a great deal more REM sleep than older children or adults. They speculated that REM sleep in newborns reflects the activity of an endogenous mechanism that may have served to prime the extra-ocular and ocular pathways while the baby was still in utero, with nerve pathways ready to go but without the possibility of input. Such priming would presumably prevent neural degeneration of these established but otherwise unstimulated networks.

A similar, or perhaps the same, endogenous mechanism may control scanning in darkness. I feel the need for proposing such a mechanism because the contrasting behavior in unpatterned light was so striking; babies frequently lost eye control. Since the eyes come under control when a visual stimulus is available, as in Studies 3, 4, and 5, it seems likely that, in some sense, the baby gives over control of his/her search behavior to external stimuli when light is available. Or perhaps it would be more accurate to say that external stimuli serve as a marker for the center of gravity of the infant's scan behavior. When no marker is available, the eye glides toward one of the canthi where control is difficult. I suspect that the relatively uniform reports of poor eye control in newborns (there are several exceptions, such as Dayton, Jones, Aiu, Rawson, Steele, & Rose, 1964a, for example) reflect observations in which no salient edges were available for the newborn to fixate on, or these edges were outside the newborn's effective horizontal band, or beyond the baby's fairly restricted accommodative range (Haynes et al., 1965). Perhaps for an edge or stimulus to be effective in sustaining eye control, a fairly constrained set of conditions must be satisfied.

Visual Activity with Edges.   Rule 4 refers to newborn scanning when an edge is encountered. Edges appear to change the newborn's scan behavior in several ways. First, the center-of-gravity of the newborn's fixations is shifted to coincide with the location of the edge. Second, the characteristics of the scan activity change: The dispersion of fixations on an axis perpendicular to the edge decreases while that parallel to the edge increases. Whereas the increase in parallel-axis distribution is minor for vertical edges it is quite large for horizontal edges. Additionally, the average size of eye movement increases primarily because processing eye movements, those which cross the edge, are larger along the horizontal component of movement.

Two elaborations on the statement regarding edge scanning are needed. First, the effectiveness of an edge is diminished greatly as that stimulus is moved vertically away from the natural resting location of the newborn's eye (the infant's central visual field). Thus, there is a narrow horizontal band or window within which the newborn responds. My guess is that this window is about 18° high, centered at the resting location of the eye (or ±9° around visual center). Kessen et al. (1972) presented a horizontal bar 12° below visual center (18° below geometric-field center) and found no response by the newborn at all to it. In the fifth study, the portions of the vertical bars above and below 9° from visual center produced little scanning activity, even though several earlier studies demonstrated the attractiveness of appropriately placed vertical edges and bars.

Detection of these components did not appear to be the problem. Most newborns in the Kessen et al. study looked near the horizontal bars but did not stay near them. In Study 5, many newborns fixated the vertical component beyond the ±9° boundaries but did not stay there, probably because once there, it was difficult for them to produce eye movements that crossed the edge. I hold that it is the high activation of neurons resulting from edge crosses or eye movements near edges that maintains scanning near them.

The Constraints on Vertical Eye Movements.   Both mechanical and neurological explanations can be offered for the newborn's greater difficulty in executing well-controlled large vertical eye movements than horizontal eye movements. Horizontal movements of each eye are produced through antagonistic action of one pair of muscles—the lateral and medial recti. These lie on a horizontal plane on either side of the eye that is virtually coincident with the horizontal meridian of the globe. Thus, all that is required for a horizontal movement is contraction of one muscle and relaxation of the other as the two other sets of extraocular muscles maintain tonus. However, the situation is more complicated for vertical eye movements. The superior and inferior rectus muscles that lie above and below the globe do not lie on a vertical plane coincident with the vertical meridian. Rather they lie on a plane about 23° off the vertical meridian with the superior oblique muscle above the globe and closer to the nasal side. Thus, simple contraction of one muscle and relaxation of the other produces an oblique and cyclotorsional movement rather than a pure vertical movement (Alpern, 1969, p. 33). (This is an oversimplification that is approximately correct when the eye is in a central position; the effect of contraction of these muscles changes with changes in the initial position of the eye.) Pure vertical movements, therefore, involve activation of at least two sets of muscles.

The mechanical complexity in production of vertical eye movements is matched by neurological complexity. A complete understanding of the higher-level neural control over eye movement is far from complete. In fact, involvement of so many cortical and subcortical areas of the brain have been implicated in eye movements that some investigators have been led virtually to conclude that primates move their eyes with their whole brain (Pasik & Pasik, 1964). However, one consistent finding from the research on eye movements in higher primates is that, whereas conjugate horizontal eye movements can be produced by unilateral brain stimulation over a wide range of areas, pure vertical eye movements are virtually never seen with unilateral stimulation (Bender & Shanzer, 1964; Crosby, Foss, & Henderson, 1952; Pasik & Pasik, 1964; Wagman, 1964). Since vertical eye movements are consistently produced only by bilateral brain stimulation, it seems reasonable to conclude that vertical eye movements require cooperating neural centers in the two hemispheres whereas horizontal eye movements do not. Perhaps the neural basis for bilateral hemispheric coöperation is not sufficiently complete in human newborns to permit pure vertical movements.

Further data suggest the independence of the horizontal and vertical eye-movement systems. Stark (1971) concluded on the basis of work on involuntary drift and corrective movements that the vertical- and horizontal-control systems are characterized by different frequency and gain components. Robinson (1970) noted that horizontal and vertical cells in the oculomotor nucleus fired independently for vertical and horizontal movements and Robinson and Fuchs (1969) proposed separate horizontal and vertical pulsers in a model of the eye-movement system.

Other behavioral evidence has been consistent with the notion not only of independence of these systems but also of greater complexity and vulnerability of the vertical-movement system. Any reduction in state of alertness tends to have its effect on first reducing the size of the vertical component, whether this be through natural-state shifts or through anesthesia (Crosby et al., 1952; Stark, 1971). It is conceivable that the absence of vertical movements in newborns reflects the presence of residual anesthesia in their system or of less than an optimal state of alertness, rather than cortical immaturity. However, given the high frequency of eye movements by our subjects and the degree of eye opening required for our recording techniques, it seems unlikely that the infants were drowsy.

I am not aware of any work on the relation between type and amount of drug administration on mothers during delivery and eye movements in the newborn. However, Jones's (1926) early work showed that horizontal tracking of visual movement occurs earlier than vertical tracking and that the advantage for horizontal tracking extended well beyond the newborn period; so the advantage of the horizontal system does not appear to be transitory or limited to the postnatal period. On the other hand, psychologists interested in diagnostic indicators of drug levels in young infants might well consider eye-movement parameters. Kron, Stein, and Goddard (1966) used sucking activity as an indicator of appropriateness of drug levels for newborns who were under withdrawal treatment for addictions transferred to them by their mothers. Eye-movement behavior might be considered as an additional indicator of central-nervous integrity in these babies.

The Effects of Experience with Particular Stimuli. One might wonder whether the greater frequency and extent of horizontal over vertical eye movements would have perceptual consequences. Horizontal eye movements might be expected to facilitate the detection of vertical stimuli, and vertical eye movements, horizontal stimuli. One perhaps could argue that the detection of vertical edges (those perpendicular to the horizon) is somehow more important than the detection of horizontal edges. Thus, the bilateral organization of the eyes, the greater horizontal than vertical extent of the visual field, the horizontal-oblique shape of the acuity function (Harrington, 1964), and the greater extent and frequency of horizontal eye movements might be seen as adaptive.

On the basis of recent research on cortical analyzers these considerations might also suggest a bias in favor of vertical detectors. Whereas the evidence suggests no preponderance of analyzers for any one orientation of edges over any other in the visual cortex of cats at birth (Hubel & Wiesel, 1963) or in adulthood (Hubel & Wiesel, 1962), there is substantial evidence that extensive early experience with particular edge orientations results in more analyzers that are sensitive to those orientations (Barlow, Narasimhan, & Rosenfeld, 1972; Blakemore & Cooper, 1970; Hirsch & Spinelli, 1970; Pettigrew & Freeman, 1973). Furthermore, there is some evidence that as visual function has become increasingly encephalized through evolution, the plasticity of analyzers to adapt to perceptual experience has also increased (Mize & Murphy, 1973).

Work with astigmatic adults has suggested that stimuli aligned with the axis of best focus produce greater neurological activity and are better discriminated even after optical correction, supporting the notion that experience has resulted in more detectors of stimuli in the favored orientation (Freeman, Mitchell, & Millodot, 1972; Freeman & Thibos, 1973). Annis and Frost (1973) further demonstrated that this effect is not limited to humans with ocular abnormalities; whereas adults raised in carpentered environments supplied the typically larger evoked potentials to presentation of vertical and horizontal edges than to diagonals, Cree Indians, raised in a noncarpentered environment did not. Thus, early experience of humans with visual forms may very well affect the perceptibility of some orientations over others; the newborn's tendency to seek stimuli may satisfy the "need" of cortical visual analyzers to receive direction from visual input.

The literature regarding greater perceptibility of vertical stimuli, though certainly suggestive, is not totally convincing. Rats perform more accurately in discrimination tasks with vertical stimuli than with horizontal stimuli

(Fitts, Mizer, Rappaport, Anderson, & Leonard, 1956), as do monkeys (Wilson & Riesen, 1966), children (Wohlwill & Wiener, 1964), and, perhaps, sharks. (My only knowledge concerning this question comes from a television program narrated by Jacques Cousteau.) However, the evoked potential work reveals only a slight, if any, advantage of vertical over horizontal gratings (Annis & Frost, 1973; Freeman & Thibos, 1973; Maffei & Campbell, 1970). We know virtually nothing about the degree of plasticity, the timing characteristics, or any of the other important parameters relating early visual experience to later perceptual development in humans. Such information is needed to guide practical decisions, for example, such as when and how much stimulation should be provided for premature infants who sometimes spend a substantial amount of time in a visually deprived atmosphere.

Contour Density, Stimulus Capture, and Form Sensitivity.   Rule 5 is concerned with the dispersion of fixations perpendicular to an edge and suggests a principle that governs *how* a stimulus is scanned. Consider first the available data. Salapatek and Kessen (1966), reported that fixation dispersion was strikingly reduced when newborns scanned a solid equilateral triangle in comparison to their scanning of a patternless field. However, Kessen et al. (1972) reported no stable reduction in fixation dispersion when a linear vertical edge was presented. The data from the studies reported in the earlier chapters suggested a small effect on the distribution of fixations along the axis perpendicular to the orientation of the edges and bars. In Studies 3 and 4 dispersion was slightly smaller in three of four cases (no difference in the fourth case) when the bars and edges were presented than during blank-field control periods. In Study 5, both axes of fixation were perpendicular to stimuli and, again, dispersion along both axes was reduced slightly. There are no other data that bear directly on this question with newborns. However, there are related data that could reflect the effect of contour density on fixation dispersion; infants in the early weeks tend either to fixate only one stimulus in a multistimulus array and to fixate single stimuli for an inordinately long period (Ames & Silfen, 1965; Horowitz, Paden, Bhana, & Self, 1972; Stechler & Latz, 1966). This phenomenon has been referred to as "attentional capture" of infants by stimuli, a phenomenon by which infants seem to be almost paralyzed or enraptured by a stimulus.

All of these data on fixation dispersion may be accommodated by assuming that, for newborns, there is an inverse relation between local contour density and fixation dispersion. Karmel (1969) and McCall and Kagan (1967) have also suggested that contour density or amount of contour is a critical parameter affecting preferences for visual stimuli by older infants. Of course, I argue that "preference" is not involved; rather, greater contour density produces a tighter scan that, incidentally, results in more fixations or longer looking time. Additionally, I believe that neither the average contour density nor the total amount of contour in a stimulus is the crucial factor for newborns. Rather, the critical factor, in many cases related to these two variables, is the relative opportunity the newborn has to scan in areas in which successive fixations can be made that displace a given number of contours near the fovea. The reason for this claim is based on a neurophysiological argument that will be offered in Chapter 9. However, the term "local contour density" was chosen to refer to the density of contours in subregions of a stimulus array.

The blank fields used for control periods provided no local areas of contour; consequently, fixation dispersion was relatively large. The edges used in the Kessen et al. study and in Study 3 provided at least one contour more than a blank field. Fixation dispersion (along the axis perpendicular to the axis of stimulus orientation) was reduced a small amount for both the horizontal and vertical edge. It might be expected that the bars in Study 4 would have had still a stronger effect than edges on fixation dispersion because two contours were available. However, the two contours of the bar were 14° apart. Given that the average eye movement was about 7° in Study 4 and that the position of the eye was usually some distance to the side of a contour before an eye movement, the bar did not provide substantial opportunity for successive fixations to displace the two available contours near the fovea. Thus, the slight reduction of variance along the X-axis for vertical bars is understandable.

My decision to exclude any provision for element or form perception in the Rule System, even in light of the Salapatek and Kessen findings with angles, was based partly on parsimony but mostly on the findings from Study 5. When a 90° angle was presented to the newborn, I found no striking tendency for the angle to be scanned more than the bars, and I observed only a slight reduction in fixation distribution—about that obtained in Studies 3 and 4. An interpretation of the occurrence of a strong angle effect in the Salapatek and Kessen study, but a weak, if any, effect in Study 5, was offered in Chapter 7 and illustrated in Fig. 7.1. To reiterate, the 60° angle in the Salapatek & Kessen study offered more opportunity for fixations that project two edges near the fovea than the right angle did in Study 5. I am claiming that the primary factor that constrains newborn scanning in an area is the number of contours that can be successively relocated on the retina near the fovea as the baby scans that area. Fig. 7.1 suggests that the eye can be moved to more locations near the 60° angle that successively displace two contours near the fovea than is the case for the 90° angle.

Finally, one can imagine that the phenomenon of "stimulus capture" that investigators have reported in the literature when they have used relatively gross observation of the eyes could, in fact, reflect a very constrained fixation distribution produced by contour-rich stimulus fields. Certainly, the observation that young infants move their eyes almost every half-second, made with more refined techniques, does not fit the concept of "stimulus capture" as that notion has been used to imply passive trapping of the baby by a stimulus. Certainly, it is doubtful that one could appreciate the newborn's detailed scanning of one angle of a triangle stimulus, as found in the Salapatek and Kessen study, by using unaided observation alone.

In summary, Rule 5 specifies a reduction in scanning proportional to resolvable local contour density, up to a point. It helps us to understand relatively broad scanning by newborns in unpatterned light, the slight reduction in perpendicular-scan variance when an edge or bar is presented (Studies 3, 4, and 5), the striking reduction in scanning of a 60° angle (Salapatek & Kessen, 1966), the less dramatic reduction in scanning of a 90° angle (Study 5), and reports in the literature of stimulus capture in the very young infant (Ames & Silfen, 1965; Horowitz et al., 1972; Stechler & Latz, 1966). I see no need to assume that newborns possess a preference hierarchy for form elements or forms. However, a direct test of Rule 5 has not been made. What is needed is a comparison of newborn scanning over stimuli that have varying amounts of contour. Pipp (1978) has just completed a relevant dissertation in my laboratory that indicates that reductions in both scan variance and in eye-movement size are correlated with increases in local contour density.

9 Maximization of Neural Firing Rate: The Principle Controlling the Newborn's Visual Activity

The rule system comprises a set of instructions the newborn obeys as the baby encounters various visual situations. There is the need to ask whether these "rules" can be understood in terms of higher-order principles that they might serve. In my view, it is likely that such a principle or principles would make adaptive biological sense and would treat scanning as an activity that reflects the operation of the whole visual system.

As such, it is the functioning of the whole system that must be addressed, not the individual eye movements. Thus, the organizing principles can not be at the level, for example, of a peripheral stimulus attracting each new fixation, followed by satiation, and then a new fixation, and the like. Behavioral observations concur with the inadequacy of this level of explanation. Fixations occur much faster than the newborn's reaction time for an eye movement to peripheral stimuli even under the most ideal circumstances (for example, see Aslin & Salapatek, 1975; Harris & MacFarlane, 1974), and, as with the adult, many fixations are "meaningless" and not under the control of visual stimuli. Thus, we need a description that accommodates the characteristics of a system partially under the control of biological constraints and partially under the control of stimulus constraints. The further need is to describe what makes that system work.

I suppose the most dramatic findings of the research presented earlier—active scanning in darkness and "preplanning" of processing eye movements—nagged at me in suggesting that the newborn might be trying to accomplish something by his/her visual activity. Although I (Haith, 1973) hinted at the possibility in a Society for Research in Child Development paper in 1968—that the newborn was wired to maintain a high level of retinal

106

stimulation—the full potential of that notion only became obvious to me through the years as I grew more aware of the single-unit work carried on in the visual cortex of infrahumans and as the rule system took shape. The idea is fairly straightforward: The newborn's visual-scanning activity is adapted to keep the firing rate of visual cortical neurons at a high level. It is rather startling how well this simple principle can account for what we have learned in the studies presented here. Moreover, visual phenomena can be accommodated that I did not originally attempt to explain, and this principle, served by the rule system, makes exceptionally good biological sense. In fact, it is not difficult to understand through the postulation of this one principle every important visual activity and development in early infancy of which we are aware.

This chapter begins by stating first the facts we must account for in any satisfactory explanatory system of newborn scanning. I then provide a brief overview of what is known about the visual system of mature higher mammals. A discussion of the neural mechanisms available to the newborn follows. Finally, I show how the postulation of a guiding principle of maximization of cortical firing rate can account for the data I have presented as well as other major facts known about early-infant vision.

VISUAL INCLINATIONS AND ACQUISITIONS
IN EARLY INFANCY

Although we are far from a complete understanding or even cataloguing of visual activity in early infancy there are certain things we know that occur at or near birth and other essential developments that take place in the first several weeks. To date, investigators have either ignored these phenomena as deserving of explanation or have not attempted a consistent explanation of them. I am concerned in the following with very basic questions and a general conceptual system that can account for them:

1. Why does a baby actively scan his/her visual field?
2. Why does a baby look at a contour or edge—that is, position the eyes so the stimulus projects to a location near the fovea?
3. Why does a baby engage in a scan that results in frequent crossing of contours or relocations of contour on the retina near the center of the eye?
4. Why does a baby engage in scanning activity that is more highly localized or less diffuse in some cases than others?

These questions derive from the studies I have reported here. However, there are other questions about the early acquisition of visual skills that should also be asked:

5. How does a baby acquire the ability to focus (accommodate) stimuli on the retina at varying distances?

6. How does a baby learn to coordinate his two eyes to obtain binocular vision?

Because I refer to recent work on visual-system function to provide answers to these questions, it is useful to review the salient aspects of the visual system now. However, the informed reader may want to skip directly to page 113.

OVERVIEW OF VISUAL SYSTEM FUNCTION

Visual activity begins in the rods and cones of the retina where photopigments are bleached by photons of light energy. Chemical changes produced by this bleaching process give rise to electrical activity that is communicated, through a set of synapses, to cortical and subcortical levels.

At the approximate center of the retina, which I have designated in the studies presented as corresponding to the fixation point, lies a dense circular cluster of cones corresponding to about 2° of visual angle. With increasing distance from this rod-free foveal area, rod density increases and cone density decreases so that far peripheral parts of the retina are cone-free.

Rod and cone photopigments differ as do their neural connections to higher centers; visual activity produced by rods is referred to as scotopic function, and that by cones, photopic function. The scotopic system is best-suited for operation in dim light and for spatial orientation and localization. The photopic system is best suited for fine-detail analysis and for detection of color.

The rods and cones synapse to a second layer of the retina to horizontal, amacrine, and bipolar cells where a substantial amount of interaction between cells occurs. These cells then synapse to ganglion cells that carry impulses to the lateral geniculate body of the thalamus. The lateral geniculate body, in turn, projects to at least visual area 17 (the striate cortex), visual area 18, and probably visual area 19. There is also evidence to suggest a projection to the inferotemporal cortex. These projections are retinotopic in organization in that locational relations are preserved. However, the rod-free foveal area occupies a disproportionately large area of each of the projection sites; this disproportionate relation is referred to as cortical magnification of the foveal area. Beside the projection of the ganglion fibers to the lateral geniculate, ganglion cells also project to the superior colliculus, except for 7° around the foveal area; this area projects directly only to the visual cortex (Crosby & Henderson, 1948; Mettler, 1964; Wilson & Toyne, 1970). The superior colliculus does receive downward cortical projections from this part of the fovea as well as from more peripheral areas; the area of superior colliculus serving the foveal region is, as in all other cases, disproportionately large.

A striking difference in neural circuitry connecting retina to higher centers exists between rods and cones. Whereas cones in the foveal area typically bear a 1:1 relation to ganglion fibers, there is an average convergence of 125 rods to each ganglion cell. Thus, the firing of a set of foveal cone cells produces firing of more cortical cells than does the firing of an equivalent set of rod cells.

Significant breakthroughs in understanding of the functional physiology of various components of the visual system have been made in the last decade or so, and this area is still one of the most active ones in psychology. Although many cone cells connect on a one-to-one basis with ganglion cells, their activity is influenced by neighboring cells. In fact, local interaction between cells plays a major role in the coding of stimuli.

A model of the activity of neurons has been developed from Hartline's (1938, 1969) and Ratliff's (Ratliff & Hartline, 1959) work on the retinal units—ommatidia—of the limulus. A single ommatidium, stimulated by light, produces neural firing in relation to the amount of light falling on it (see Fig. 9.1). It is important to note also that the firing rate is higher at the onset of the stimulus than it is later when the rate settles down to a maintenance level.

An example of retinal interaction, lateral inhibition, is given in Fig. 9.2. The rate of impulses produced by a single illuminated cell is quite high (left of figure), is slowed by illumination of surrounding cells (center), and then recovers again when the neighborhood illumination is removed (right). Thus, cells can exert suppressive influences on neighboring cells.

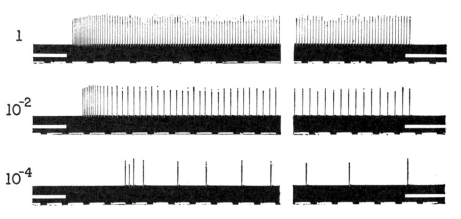

FIG. 9.1.   Record of the discharge of nerve impulses in a single optic nerve, from the eye of a limulus stimulated by illumination of the facet associated with its receptor. Relative light intensity is shown at the left. Time markers at bottom show .2-second intervals. Light onset is indicated by blackening of white band above time markers (modelled after Hartline, 1969, Fig. 1, p. 271).

FIG. 9.2.   Illustration of inhibition in the eye of the limulus. The firing activity
from a receptor, produced by steady illumination is slowed when a group of 20
to 30 neighboring receptors, in a surrounding region, are illuminated. The time
markers at the bottom of the record indicate .2-second time intervals. The
blackened white band, just above the time markers indicates the period of
illumination of neighboring cells (modelled after Hartline, 1969, Fig. 6, p. 273).

The time parameters and relative degree of influence of inhibitory and
excitatory effects are shown in Fig. 9.3. The neighboring cells are at first
simultaneously and equally illuminated by the same intensity light throughout the experiment. However, cell 1, whose firing rate is described by the open
circles, is illuminated by a brighter light at time 0. Note the large burst in firing
rate of cell 1, which then falls to a lower maintained rate. There is also a

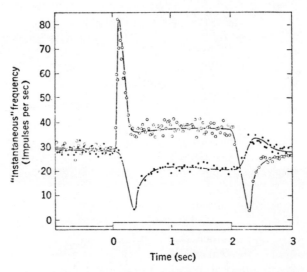

FIG. 9.3.   Illustration of simultaneous excitatory and inhibitory effects in two
adjacent receptor units in the lateral eye of the limulus. One receptor unit,
whose firing rate is indicated by filled dots, was illuminated steadily
throughout the period shown. The other unit was illuminated steadily until
time 0 when a large increase in illumination occurred, where it remained for 2
seconds. A large burst of firing appeared in the more strongly illuminated cell,
accompanied by a sharp decrement in the neighboring cell. Both cells settled
down to a moderated ambient-firing level until the more brightly illuminated
cell was returned to its original intensity value. The relations in firing rate
between the two cells temporarily reversed (modelled after Ratliff, 1961, Fig.
10, p. 197).

smaller transient inhibition of cell 2, which takes somewhat longer, reflecting a well-known tendency for inhibitory effects to act somewhat more slowly than excitatory ones. After the transient, cell 2 then maintains a firing rate well above the peak level but still below the original ambient level. When the illumination on cell 1 is reduced to the baseline level, there is a transient decrease in the firing of cell 1 accompanied by an increase—or release from inhibition—of cell 2, followed by a return of both to the base level.

Hartline (1969) summarizes the role of inhibitory interaction in vision:

> One role is enhancement of contrast. Strongly excited receptor elements in brightly lighted regions of the retinal image exert a stronger inhibition on receptors in more dimly lighted regions than the latter exert on the former. Thus the disparity in the action of the receptors is increased, and contrast enhanced. Since inhibition is stronger between close neighbors than between widely separated ones, steep intensity gradients in the retinal image—edges and contours—will be accentuated by contrast [p. 273].

This crispening of contours, whose psychological effect is to make white seem whiter and black seem blacker near a black-white edge than elsewhere, is known as "simultaneous contrast," analogous to Mach bonds (Ratliff, 1965).

The model of optic-nerve activity developed from studies on the horse-shoe crab appears to apply equally well to geniculate-cell activity in higher mammals. Up to the level of the lateral-geniculate body, cells have an excitatory-center, inhibitory-surround, receptive-field organization (Kuffler, 1953). (The receptive field of a cell is defined as that area in the visual field over which a point source can affect the cell's firing rate.) Most cells in the lateral-geniculate body increase in firing rate either when light or darkness falls near the center of their receptive field and decrease firing rate when the same input falls outside this central excitatory area, but still within the bounds of the receptive field.

Single-unit recording of cell activity in the visual cortex has yielded a somewhat different picture. In cats and monkeys cells do not have a center-surround organization; rather, the excitatory regions of cells have a linear organization frequently flanked by inhibitory regions (Hubel & Wiesel, 1959, 1962). Apparently, several geniculate cells with center-surround fields converge onto single visual-cortex cells, thereby providing a stage of coding of sensory information. The linear organization of the receptive fields, with accompanying inhibitory flanks, makes these cells especially sensitive to the orientation of an edge in the receptive field. Several types of cells have been described. Simple cells have small receptive fields and are especially sensitive to the precise orientation, location, and brightness relation of the two sides of a slit if it has flanking inhibitory regions, or to an edge if it possesses a side-by-side arrangement. Simple cells are not found outside of area 17 and appear to be especially dense in layer 4 of the cortex, the primary projection layer for the LGN fibers. Simple cells are of greatest concern to us here as my speculations relate to area 17, an area that is well advanced in newborns compared to other visual areas and most other areas of the brain (Conel, 1939).

A second type of cell has been described, the complex cell, which does not possess the strict limitations on position characteristic of the simple cell, though it also is orientation specific. Cells in this category may be especially sensitive to edges or particular slit widths, but will respond well to "preferred" stimuli placed in a wide range of areas of the visual field. Complex cells are found in areas 17 and 18 and are thought to receive impulses from several simple cells that have common receptive-field axes.

Hubel and Wiesel (1962) also described cells that they called lower-order hypercomplex and higher-order complex. These cells also had specific receptive-field axes. In addition, the lower-order cells responded best to particular lengths of edges, slits, or bars, whereas the higher-order cells responded best to more complex stimuli, such as angles. These more complex cells were found most frequently in areas 18 and 19 in the more superficial layers of the cortex, areas that are poorly developed in the newborn brain (Conel, 1939).

Virtually all cell types were sensitive to movement. As with the response of the ommatidium, described earlier, the appearance of a preferred stimulus in the receptive field typically produces a burst of firing that settles down to a lower ambient rate. Hubel and Wiesel (1962) suggested that the effect of a moving stimulus for a simple cell may be synergistic. As a contour moves into the receptive field, first stimulating the inhibitory region and then the excitatory region, there is a simultaneous excitation and release of inhibition resulting in a large transient effect. To this point, I have only discussed the effects of stimulation of one eye. But there are strong binocular effects of stimulation.

About 80% of all cells in the visual cortex of cats are affected by stimulation of the preferred orientation in either eye at corresponding retinal locations (Hubel & Wiesel, 1959, 1962). Simultaneous stimulation produced substantially more firing of these cells than stimulation of either eye alone. On the other hand, if the stimuli were slightly out of register in the two eyes, an overall suppression of firing occurred, resulting in less activity than if one eye alone were stimulated. Whereas all cell types in the cat were binocularly receptive, simple cells in layer 4 of the monkey's visual cortex were only monocularly receptive (Hubel & Wiesel, 1968). However, as in the cat, most complex cells in the monkey cortex were binocular.

As would be expected from the principle of lateral inhibition, image focus on the retina is important. As focus decreases, the contour gradient is spread over a greater pool of cells and the effects of lateral inhibition decrease. In the limiting case a homogeneous brightness results, and such a field has only minor effects on cortical-cell activity. Apparently, some cells are hypersensitive to contour crispness. Hubel and Wiesel (1962) reported that one cell could not be activated by the image of a projected edge, although it did respond to black tape placed in the same position. Apparently, the light scatter produced by the projected image reduced contour sharpness below the acceptance range for that cell.

These properties of visual-system activity were reviewed because they play a major role in my account of the visual behavior of the newborn. Let me highlight those aspects that are most crucial to my argument:

1. Edges falling near the fovea activate more cortical cells than those falling in the periphery.

2. The largest burst of cortical activity occurs when an edge first falls in the receptive fields of cells.

3. The sharper the edge contrast or focus, the greater the firing effect.

4. Stimuli viewed binocularly produce much greater cortical firing when they are in register than when they are not.

5. Area 17 of the visual cortex is the primary projection site for ascending optical fibers, and layer 4 of area 17, where these fibers synapse, has a heavy concentration of simple edge and slit detectors.

FUNCTIONING OF THE
HUMAN VISUAL SYSTEM AT BIRTH

Given the basic overview of visual functioning in the preceding section, it is now pertinent to ask which aspects of this system are available to the newborn at birth. General reviews of the relevant literature have been written (Haith, 1978; Haith & Campos, 1977; Hershenson, 1967), so this is brief. I want to lay the basis here for the statement that the newborn visual system is sufficiently mature for contours to activate simple-cell detectors in the visual cortex.

At the first level, one can ask whether the newborn is sensitive to light at all. The behavioral data presented in the studies reported here confirmed the well-known fact that they are (Pratt, 1954; Kessen et al., 1970). It is generally accepted that the pupillary response to light is also present, which suggests that the newborn iris muscle responds adaptively, if sluggishly, by birth (Mann, 1964). However, Duke-Elder and Cook (1963) held that the dilator "muscle is not functionally active until after birth [p. 305]," resulting in a small pupil. Perhaps confusion over this question reflected difficulty in observing pupil size in the newborn over a wide range of light levels. Our techniques permitted permanent recording of pupil size in situations ranging from absolute darkness to a moderate light level. We observed very clear adaptive pupillary changes over this range that leaves no doubt in my mind that the pupillary response is strong at birth. In fact, pupillary constriction in light and dilation in darkness were so obvious that it prevented us, in Studies 1 and 2, from obtaining pure blind judgments on the observational variables, and it should be remembered that our light levels were moderate indeed.

Proceeding along the light path, I next ask whether the newborn can produce a focused image on the retina through accommodation of the lens. Little work has been done in this area. Haynes et al. (1965) used dynamic retinoscopy to establish that the newborn is not capable of variable accommodation; the lens appeared to be fixed at a median distance of about 19 cm and gradually became more adaptable over the first 3 months of life. On the other hand, evidence was offered that the system is not passive: During sleep lens shape was different than during wakefulness. Hershenson (1970) has questioned these data on the basis that the object for fixation used by Haynes et al. may have been insufficiently attractive for radial tracking to occur.

An additional problem is that accommodative readings can be taken only when the eye is still; as we have seen, newborns normally move their eyes at least twice every second when they are in an alert state. It may be the case that the young infants in the Haynes et al. study were in a momentary open-eyed trance when readings were taken. Even if the data of Haynes et al. are correct, the newborn is capable of producing a focused image on the retina for stimuli at a distance of 19 cm or so.[1] Closer or farther stimuli would become increasingly more defocused as the distance from this focal plane increased. Estimates of visual acuity at birth average around 20/200 to 20/300, which corresponds to moderate-strong nearsightedness in the uncorrected eye (Dobson & Teller, 1978). However, people who have such defective vision can very easily identify most objects in the out-of-focus visual field. The definition of 20/300 vision is detection of a separation of two edges that are separated by 1/4° of arc; this corresponds to the ability to detect a separation of 1 inch at a 20 ft. distance. Too frequently investigators have assumed that the newborn's optical apparatus does not permit the baby to see anything in front of or behind the newborns's supposedly fixed plane of accommodation; obviously this is not true.

Once an image is formed on the retina, we can ask how well the photoreceptors, rods and cones, are equipped to carry this information to the brain. There is substantial disagreement and inconsistency in the literature on this point. Authoritative references in the field of retinal embryology maintain that the macular region of the retina is advanced in development over the peripheral regions through the first trimester of fetal life. After that

---

[1]Salapatek (1975) suggested that the lens, in fact, may be adaptable to varying distances, but that the young infants' neural structures may be insufficiently mature to respond to the high spatial frequencies by which fine lens tuning is accomplished.

period, the peripheral regions of the retina catch up and reach a fairly complete stage of development by birth. However, the macular region is believed to continue developing through at least the first 4 months of life (Duke-Elder & Cook, 1963; Mann, 1964). These sources hold that at birth the ganglion and bipolar cells (together about five layers thick) still lie directly in front of the macula in the light path to the fovea and have not begun to slope to the side to create the foveal depression, as in the adult. Only one cone-nucleus layer is held to exist at birth, and "the cones themselves are short and ill-developed, a circumstance which helps to explain the absence of fixation at birth" (Duke-Elder & Cook, 1963, p. 98). And Mann (1964) concurs that the cone nuclei form a single row at the center of the fovea,

> but have increased to two and sometimes three rows at the periphery of the macula. The cones themselves do not yet appear any longer than their fellows in the paracentral regions. This arrangement demonstrates the anatomical reason for the well-known clinical fact that the power of central fixation is not present at birth [p. 115].

Early research on the development of retinal voltage changes to light stimulation, using electroretinography, confirmed the idea of a nonfunctional macula at birth. Flashes of white light normally produce a short-latency, negative a-wave followed by a longer-latency, positive b-wave in the mature retina. The a-wave is related to photopic vision, mediated by cones, and the b-wave to scotopic vision mediated by rods. Newborn ERGs were characterized by the existence of only the scotopic b-wave (Zetterström, 1951, 1955). Duke-Elder and Cook (1963) placed great emphasis on this deficit in newborns and related it to other visual deficiencies in newborn vision, from which it seemed likely that many people assumed that the newborn visual system is substantially immature.

> As would be expected, the full development of the visual reflexes is delayed until their anatomical basis is established. A fixation reflex is present at birth, but it is only feebly developed, responding momentarily to a strong stimulus such as a bright light; initially the movements of the eyes are independent, irregular and unconjugated. . . . By the age of 5 to 6 weeks the conjugate reflex is sufficiently developed to allow the two eyes to follow a light over a considerable range [p. 305].

Questions have been raised about the data base that was used for early statements about the morphology of the newborn retina, and findings based on modern behavioral and physiological techniques have cast doubt on many of these opinions. An examination of the data from which Mann made her inferences raises doubts about its validity; apparently, many of Duke-Elder and Cook's comments are based on Mann's and, hence, the same data base.

As far as I and others who have investigated the issue (Salapatek et al., 1972) can tell, the data on retinal development were based on a few babies who died for unknown reasons in the late 1800s. There is no assurance that these babies devleoped normally to the point at which they died; development may very well have been retarded, in which case the retinae examined would have been abnormally immature and not representative of normal newborns.

Ordy, Samorajski, Collins, and Nagy (1965) carried out an elegant study of retinal development in rhesus monkeys from birth using electroretinography, fundus photography, histology, electron microscopy, and behavioral tests for visual acuity. These data are relevant because the rhesus monkey's visual system is reasonably comparable to the human's. Judging from a wide variety of measures of visual function, such as ERG, VER, eye opening, visual acuity, and differentiation of brain cells, the maturity of the human visual system at birth seems roughly equivalent to that of the rhesus monkey and more advanced than that of the kitten (Ellingson, 1964; Horsten & Winkelman, 1962, 1964; Rose & Ellingson, 1970; Rose, 1971; Wiesel & Hubel, 1974). The newborn monkey retina shows clear evidence of advanced thinning of the ganglion and bipolar layers in front of the macula and several layers of cone nuclei. Electron microscopy revealed well-differentiated inner- and outer-cone segments and well-developed lamellar bimembraneous folding sacs (Ordy et al., 1965). The outer segments of rods and cones have been held to be the last element to differentiate, sometime after birth. Although generalization from monkey to human is hazardous, there are data suggesting that the visual system of the human may be even more advanced. Studies of the VER in humans have established that the primary and secondary waves of the evoked response are identifiable at birth (Ellingson, 1964). Monkeys, kittens, and rabbits, in that order, develop the primary component of the VER somewhat later (Ellingson, 1964). Thus, one would suspect, at the least, that the anatomical maturity of the human fovea would not be substantially behind that of the rhesus.

Research on the ERG in the early 1960s demonstrated the a-wave of the ERG in the newborn through the use of dark adaptation and brighter light flashes (Horsten & Winkelman, 1962, 1964). Additionally, the x-wave component of the ERG, a response to colored light that only the photopic system could mediate, has been discovered (Barnet et al., 1965). Additional evidence of foveal functioning is offered by data on photic following at rates of up to 72 flashes per minute (Horsten & Winkelman, 1964), thought to be too fast for scotopic vision, estimates of newborn visual acuity as great as 7.5′ (Dayton et al., 1964a), and my own data, presented here, that indicate that fixation near edges occurs a substantial portion of the viewing time. Thus, there is relatively solid evidence that the fovea is functional at birth at least at some level. This is not to say, of course, that further development does not occur; pigmentation of the retina is far from complete at birth; the bipolar and ganglion layers must thin out further; the cone nuclei become longer and more slender; the latencies of ERG components decreases. But the evidence suggests that the newborn is not afoveal.

Finally, there is disconfirming evidence concerning many of the early behavioral claims regarding newborn visual immaturity. Fixation has been elicited from stimuli less obtrusive than a bright light. Saccadic movements and fixations have many of the characteristics of adult activity. Movements of the eyes in the alert newborn are normally not independent and they are usually conjugate (Dayton et al., 1964a; Hershenson, 1964; McGinnis, 1930; Wickelgren, 1967). Light or dots are followed at birth (Blanton, 1917; Dayton et al., 1964b; Haith, 1966).

Since development of the visual system proceeds from inside out with the end organs the last to develop, evidence of some maturity of all components of the retina suggests that components further along the line should be functional. The data support this interpretation. In the kitten, for example, even before the eyes normally open and the visual-evoked response can be obtained from retinal stimulation, thalamocortical activity can be detected through stimulation of the lateral-geniculate nucleus (Purpura, 1971).

Rose and Ellingson (1970) point out the relation between behavioral, physiological, and anatomical data in the kitten.

Initially when apical axodendritic connections are developing, only a long-latency negative wave [of the visually evoked response] is present, and there is no visual behavioral activity in the kitten; the eyes first open at ten to twelve days of age. During the second ten days, when the basilar dendrites and axosomatic connections mature and the shorter latency positive-negative component develops, the kitten manifests initial following (at 14 days—approximately 2 to 4 days after the eyes open). Between nine and fifteen days, electrocortical sensory arousal first appears [p. 429].

As mentioned earlier, the shorter-latency, specific negative-positive and longer-latency diffuse negative components of the VER are both present in the human newborn.

The shorter-latency component presumably reflects activation along the thalamocortical pathway (Anohkin, 1961; Purpura, 1961; Rose & Lindsley, 1968; Scheibel, 1962; Scheibel & Scheibel, 1961). Because the more mature early component of the VER is present in human newborns, one might expect from Rose's observations on kittens that electrocortical sensory arousal and visual following should also be observable. They are (Blanton, 1917; Dayton et al., 1964b; Ellingson, 1964; Haith, 1966). Compared to the newborn kitten, the newborn human's visual apparatus seems quite sophisticated. If these considerations regarding the anatomical and physiological underpinnings of the VER are correct, then the widely accepted notion that the newborn is a decorticate (for example, Bronson, 1974) is puzzling indeed, at least for the visual system. Data presented by Rakic (1974) suggest that the cortical-cell components of the primate visual system are laid down well before birth, and Conel's (1939) classic studies of the newborn visual cortex suggest it is among the most advanced portions of the brain.

The status of visual analyzers at birth is an open question. Again I am forced to point to the subhuman data. Hubel and Wiesel (1963) studied kittens at 8, 16, 19, and 20 days using single-unit recording techniques in area 17 and found no substantial age difference in the specificity of responsiveness of cells to edge orientation. Although the data suggest that the retinal portion of the retino-thalamo-cortical paths was not functional in the youngest kittens, adult-like simple- and complex-cell activity was obtained with two exceptions. The cells were less orientation specific and the response of cells of the newborn were much less brisk than for the adult. However, eye-dominance patterns, the columnar organization of receptive fields, and binocular receptivity of cells were all found to be similar to that of the adult.

Given the greater maturity of the human-newborn visual system than the kitten at birth, it would appear that as much development would be observable in the human if recordings could be obtained. In line with this reasoning, recent work on newborn rhesus monkeys suggests cortical-cell responsivity that looks more mature than in the kitten (Wiesel & Hubel, 1974).

In the preceding discussion, I have tried to establish the basis for the following, relatively conservative, conclusion. There is reason to believe that the anatomical and physiological components of the visual system necessary for activating simple cells in the visual cortex are functionally adequate at some level in the normal human newborn.

10 How the Newborn's Scanning System Works: Explanation and Clarification

Where does this review and speculation about newborn-human visual functioning take us? Recall my claim that the newborn's visual activity can be understood in terms of a system that serves to keep visual cortical-firing rate at a high level. I have now reviewed literature that makes that claim at least a possibility in terms of the requisite neurophysiological and anatomical hardware. Now we can consider how the various facts of visual activity fit this notion.

First, it is necessary to introduce two scanning routines that serve the function of keeping firing rate at a high-level—an Ambient Search Routine (ASR) and an Inspection Scan Routine (ISR). The ASR serves to find targets for inspection. It governs the continuous activity of the eye-movement system and gains predominant control over eye-movement activity when the cortical-firing rate is low. The ISR is called into play when a target is detected and it produces contour encounters and crosses. Obviously, if two routines control eye movements there must be some competition. The data best fit the notion that, to the extent the ISR produces a high firing rate, the ASR is suppressed. It is important to note that I chose the word "suppressed" rather than "inhibited." I conceive the ISR as an overlay on the ASR. The reason is that common observation and, unfortunately, experiments indicate that a lot of eye movements by newborns or, for that matter, adults are "meaningless"—not under the obvious control of visual stimuli. Newborns will often *not* look at stimuli. Adults will often look toward a wall, a blackboard, the floor, etc. during, for example, conversations. Though a bane to attempts to explain fixation patterns, these fixations do make sense if one thinks about the eye-movement generators as constantly active and as meant to serve at least one function of sampling the environment and, thereby, alerting the organism to significant events and changes in the visual field.

In a sense, then, many eye movements seem meaningless because the experimenter does not control them; they are manifestations of a continuously active biological system meant to sample the energy provided by the currently available visual array. Thus, the ISR can be thought of as a task-specific routine and the ASR as a general-sampling routine. To the extent that the task controls looking, and I claim that "control" is a function of firing rate, the ASR is constrained. If firing rate wanes, the ASR becomes more predominant and other stimuli in the field can be detected.

Now let us return to our task of accounting for the behaviors I and others have observed.

1. Fact. Newborns actively move their eyes in darkness and in homogeneously lit fields. *Interpretation:* Since uniform light produces a low cortical-firing rate no matter what the intensity level (Hubel & Wiesel, 1959), especially in the relatively "quiet" newborn cortex (Hubel & Wiesel, 1963; Purpura, 1971), the ASR produces a broad undirected scan.

2. Fact. Newborns look at stimuli (a phenomenon taken for granted that has, to date, eluded explanation). Translated, this means that newborns position their eye so that edges fall near the fovea. *Interpretation:* Since the central retina contains the densest cluster of cells, connects to relatively more cortical cells than does the periphery, and enjoys greater cortical magnification that the periphery, an edge which is projected on the central retina produces more cortical firing than on any other area.

3. Fact. Rather than simply staying near an edge, newborns attempt to cross back and forth over them. *Interpretation:* Remember that a burst of firing occurs in cortical cells when an edge is first placed in their receptive fields. Firing rate slows to a lower maintained level as inhibitory influences come into play (see Fig. 9.3). Thus, it is clear that firing rate would be enhanced by the repeated relocation of an edge on fresh pools of cells. If a gradient of excitation exists around the midpoint of the activated set of cells, the baby could also maximize firing by moving a substantial distance from his/her current position. Such a gradient could be expected if the newborn had a somewhat fuzzy image of contours, which might be produced by imperfect optical focus. Remember, however, that edges that fall near the fovea activate the largest number of cortical receptors. Thus, the question becomes, how can the baby move the eye to relocate an edge farthest from the current position but still remain near the fovea? The answer is: by crossing the edge. A diagram of the hypothesized sequence of events is shown in Fig. 10.1 for two successive fixations that fall on either side of an edge. This analysis, in

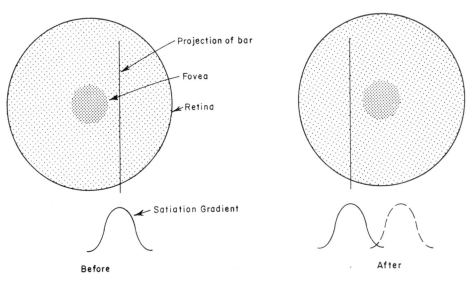

FIG. 10.1.   Model of hypothesized neural activity before and after an edge cross. Large circular zones represent retina, and central circular zone, fovea. Normal curves (bottom) indicate hypothesized gradient of adaptation of cells. An eye movement that produces a relocation of projection of edge on the opposite side of the fovea results in least overlap between cells comprising the two gradients. At the same time, projected edge remains near the cell-rich fovea.

assuming both that firing rate is best maintained when the newborn moves an edge as far as possible from the present site and when the projection of the edge is kept near the fovea, at once accommodates the finding that newborns tend to cross edges and that they cross with relatively large eye movments.[1]

4. Fact.   The fixation distribution perpendicular to the orientation of stimuli decreases only slightly in comparison to control periods when low-contour density stimuli are presented (for example, edges), but decreases strikingly when higher-contour density stimuli are presented (for example, acute angles). *Interpretation:* The more edges falling on a set of retinal receptors, the higher the resulting cortical-firing rate, especially if those edges are close enough to project simultaneously to areas near the fovea. The hypothesized interrelation between the ASR and ISR accomodates this

---

[1]I should also point out that by crossing an edge boundary and displacing the projection of that edge on the opposite hemiretina, the baby directly activates completely separate sets of cortical cells in the two different hemispheres in rapid succession. It is unlikely that cross-hemispheric connections are sufficiently mature to provide secondary activation, so the impact of this primary activation should be significant. I thank Derek Price for offering that suggestion.

finding; that is, to the extent that the ISR produces a high cortical-firing rate, the ASR will be constrained. This principle is obviously adaptive to a system that is wired to maintain a high firing rate. If current inspection activity is not producing high firing, the ASR will act to locate other, potentially more satisfying, stimuli in the visual field.

To this point, I have only dealt with the findings from my own work. However, with slight modification this scheme can also account for several other phenomena that have been reported in the literature.

5. *Fact.* Although newborn accomodation appears not to be very adaptable, by 4 months of age accommodation reaches a near-adult stage of perfection. As was the case with fixation of stimuli, accommodation and convergence (which I consider below) are phenomena whose development is simply taken for granted. *Interpretation:* We know from the animal work that, because of lateral inhibition, stimuli in sharp focus produce more firing than blurred stimuli. I alluded earlier to the observation of Hubel and Wiesel (1962) that one cell would not even fire to the projection of a black bar, whereas it did fire to a strip of black tape; photographic projections of stimuli diffuse light and blur edges to some extent. Blur in the extreme produces a homogeneous field, which does not affect cortical firing at all. The interpretation of how accommodation is acquired by a system wired to keep firing rate high is straightforward. As the lens adjusts to an increase focus, firing rate increases; as the lens adjusts to decrease focus, firing rate decreases. Thus, as the requisite musculature matures, the infant can work by a simple error-correction routine to develop proper accommodation.

6. *Fact.* Although newborn convergence is imperfect and variable, within the first few months of life stable convergence is accomplished. (Convergence should not be confused with conjugate eye movement. Newborns move their eyes conjugately most of the time.) *Interpretation:* In the visual system of normal cats, most cells of all types from simple to higher-order hypercomplex are binocular; that is, they are affected by stimulation from either eye, though one eye is usually more affected than the other. It is well established that when binocular cells are stimulated by the same visual element, in corresponding retinal locations of both eyes, they fire at a much higher rate than if stimulated by either eye alone. However, if the visual elements are out of register by a small amount, the cell's activity is suppressed, firing at an even lower rate than if only one eye were stimulated. Cortical cells appear to be tuned to fire to stimuli that correspond binocularly. Thus, once again, there is a mechanism involving cortical-firing rates that could account for a visual accomplishment in early infancy. As the eyes converge on an edge, a higher firing rate would result; as deconvergence occurs, firing rate would

decrease sharply. The system I have described should obviously "seek" convergence. It should be pointed out that simple cells found in layer 4 in the primate cortex do not respond binocularly as in the cat (Wiesel & Hubel, 1974). Perhaps binocular convergence accompanies the maturation of more complex cells in the cortex.

7. *Fact.* Very young infants tend to look at only one stimulus in a paired-stimulus array, whereas older infants look at both. The prior "interpretation" of this observation is that newborns are captured by stimuli, whereas older infants capture stimuli. *Interpretation:* It is clear that newborns are not captured by stimuli in the sense of being drawn into a hypnotic trance; they move their eyes virtually every ½ second. Stimuli that have been used in past experiments have been fairly complex, containing a high degree of contour density. Therefore, the ISR could be expected to create a high firing rate with consequent suppression of the ASR. A gross measure of orientation of the eye would not reveal the detailed inspection activity of the baby and probably lead to the mistaken impression of "stimulus capture." Similar microanalytic eye-movement activity would probably also be discovered in, for example, biochemists as they inspect specimens on slides. In short, this activity probably reflects just the opposite of what the "stimulus capture" notion implies—an intense inspection of a limited array.

Although my interpretation accounts for the absence of a broad scan over dense arrays by newborns, it does not deal with the shift to a broader scan in older infants. Frankly, I do not have a completely satisfactory answer, but the shift can be handled in two ways. The first is to claim that the system raises its requirements for cortical-firing rate. This is manifested in a shifting relation between degree of suppression of the ASR (produced by the ISR) and cortical firing, such that a given amount of suppression requires a higher firing rate than before. I "half believe" this interpretation because I think pure reafferent activation plays some role in visual scanning throughout life. However, it is also clear that such a principle, operating in isolation, would be terribly maladaptive for an older organism. And it is also clear that such factors as stimulus organization, meaning, memory, and task requirements begin to play a role in scanning as early as 2 months of age (Cornell, 1975; Fantz et al., 1975; Haith, Bergman, & Moore, 1977; Milewski, 1976; Ruff & Birch, 1974; Salapatek, 1975).

So another way of interpreting the shift is to say that the "system" is looking for something other than net cortical activation at an older age. What the ISR must produce to inhibit the ASR changes, because the infant's agenda changes with age. Unfortunately, the interpretation has to shift to a less physiological basis, but I still believe that conceptual concern should focus on how the system is organized to acquire information, rather than with the dimensions of stimuli that engage it.

THE BIOLOGICAL UTILITY OF
THE "HIGH FIRING" RATE PRINCIPLE

Of course, it is not essential that theories make adaptive sense, but it certainly does not hurt. The interpretations I have offered, to my mind, make very good biological sense. It is clear that the visual system is functional at birth, and it is well known that the maintenance of old pathways and the establishment of new connections depend on neural activation. Thus, one might have expected the newborn to be biologically prepared to seek input and to behave in a fashion that would keep neural-activation levels high. This would seem especially important in the early days of life when the baby is awake for such brief periods. It is also interesting to note that the same activity that produces a high-firing rate, fixating and scanning near areas of high contour density, is also an activity that keeps babies near the most informative parts of their visual field.

Perceptual theorists agree that homogeneous surfaces are uninformative; it is the edges and boundaries of stimuli that carry the important information. One could imagine a sequence in which babies first scan areas of high contour density for their firing potential. Such activity would facilitate neural growth and, as associative areas and memory capabilities develop, these same stimulus regions would provide information for synthesizing objects and placing them in a spatial-temporal perspective. It also seems obvious to me that it is more adaptive for a newborn to be endowed with facilities for *acquiring* information and the plasticity for adapting to the consequences of that acquisitive process, than with predetermined templates or preference hierarchies, as has been traditionally assumed. The reason is that the range of potential visual experiences that newborns could have been exposed to through the historical millennia of homo sapiens and over the geographical diversity of current humankind is so vast that virtually no presettings would be universally appropriate. And I would expect the principles of visual organization to be similar for all mammals, at least for primates.

So, we can add to these considerations the range of experiences to which newborn primates and other mammals are exposed. The theory I have proposed easily transcends these diversities, whereas a theory that proposes that some configurations, or visual dimensions, or levels of dimensions have native priority would not. In short, I am claiming that: the immature newborn's visual-neural pathways require activation for maintenance and growth; the newborn is wired to behave in a manner that keeps those pathways firing at a high level; this behavior brings him into contact with the most informative portions of the visual field; the organization of the *information-acquisition* routines are innately given, but the neural tuning for all but the simplest visual patterns (that is, edges) is acquired through experience. And, logically speaking, nature should not have done it any other way.

11 Disclaimers and Clarifications

Partly because I have lived with the data and ideas of this book for so long, and partly because so many colleagues and students have been willing to listen, to read, and to comment, I have had opportunities to learn about confusions that my claims may generate. Here I want to consider some of the issues that have been raised in colloquia, the classroom, casual conversations, and written comments on my papers by my friends.

First of all, I want to emphasize that I was not studying responses or reflexes in the research I presented, nor did I concern myself with these in the interpretations I offered. Newborns have traditionally been thought of as "reflexive," and it is natural to try to translate the activity I reported into reflexology. As I understand the term, "reflexes" are usually considered to be unconditioned, momentary, and unitary reactions to the onset of discrete stimuli. But the studies reported here employed situations and stimuli that were of lasting duration, and the behavior observed consisted of hundreds of fixations and movements as opposed to a single unitary reaction.

There may also be a tendency to think of the activity I reported as a "response" to stimulation. Certainly, hundreds of studies have been reported in which visual stimuli have been presented to babies and the duration of looking at each of the stimuli recorded. Duration of looking is often treated as a "response" to stimulation in keeping with the prevalent tradition of psychologists to think of discrete, measurable pieces of behavior as caused or controlled by stimuli. The comments in the preceding paragraph are relevant here, but it might be useful to explain more fully exactly what I was doing. We can characterize the approach I used as observational—highly technical, constrained, controlled, and instrumented—but still strictly observational. My attempt at precision and control can be misinterpreted; we usually think in terms of "stimuli" and "responses" and "judgments" in such situations. Observation is typically carried out in more natural settings. But this is not the only unusual aspect of these experiments. The data were unusual too.

Usually, experiments deal with single discrete responses and, for example, measure the latency or strength of each; or, in some cases, the frequency may be analyzed with the assumption that each event, as for example in sucking, has pretty much the same meaning. Much less frequently, psychologists examine sequences of events over time. Even then, each event is manifestly different; for example, mother picks up baby, baby tenses → mother talks → baby smiles → mother smiles → baby coos. Eye movements and fixations fall between these categories. Sequential activity was examined, yet, essentially, each "event" had the same form as all the others but probably not the same meaning. And I would argue that each event or fixation was not "determined" in the same sense that smiles and vocalizations seem to be in a mother-infant dyadic interaction. To repeat myself, many fixations have no particular relevance for the stimulus; they reflect the activity of a system that is doing its adaptive environmental-sampling "thing."

What then was I studying if not the response to stimuli or reflexes caused by stimuli? I was studying the external manifestation of an information-acquisition system, and I used measures that treated it as a system that has spatial and temporal properties. The spatial properties were captured by location- and fixation-variance measures, the temporal properties by measures of movement that were derived from fixation sequences. Finally, I proposed interpretations that are appropriate to a *system*. Eye movements and fixations were not treated individually, they were considered from a probabilistic point of view. Thus, what I was interested in was how the properties of the system changed as visual situations changed. Another phrasing might be: How do visual situations constrain the activities of the system? As I view it, the constantly active routines of scanning, used by the baby, produce feedback depending on the visual circumstance (or field). The result of this sensorimotor loop then determines the balance between the ASR and ISR, with consequent effects on the *properties* of further scanning. It is the description of these properties of the system with which I was concerned. Stimuli, then, were not seen as "causing" eye movements, they were considered to affect eye movements by constraining the *system* responsible for controlling eye movements.

One of the criticisms of the findings in darkness can be handled from this perspective. This criticism maintains that eye movements in darkness are simply random activity. This is a good example to make the point. Looking at any particular motion of the eye, or fixation, this kind of claim is hard to discredit. But if one thinks about scanning as reflecting the activity of a system, then one has to ask what a truly random system might look like. Then we can ask what nonrandomness exists and, by doing so, partially come to a description of the system itself.

Here is where the approach of talking about stimuli constraining activity rather than producing it makes the most sense. We can start with the assumption of a living, hence active, system. The "organization" of this system can be described in terms of nonentropy. The constraints are produced both by biological structure and by adaptations to stimulus circumstances. The structure then refers to restrictions on randomness. One can see a clear analogue here to the approach used in systems theory (Von Bertalanffy, 1968), and I think the analogy is quite appropriate.

To begin at the simplest level, the eyes do not rotate 360°, nor do they roll down the cheeks, nor do they move independently, and they move more along the horizontal axis than the vertical axis. These facts reflect neuromuscular constraints on randomness. Just as there are neuromuscular constraints, there appear also to be behavioral ones; eye movements in darkness are almost always in control, are smooth, terminate in sharp fixations, are small, and usually located near the center of the field. These very constraints on "randomness" describe the system, and this is the level of analysis I am concerned with. The *direction* of eye movement from one moment to the next, or the place at which the eye comes to rest, may be indeterminate to a large extent, but that is a characteristic of the system, too—one which I feel can be explained.

Even when stimuli are presented, I doubt if many fixations are generated on a fixation-by-fixation basis, and I am certain not all are. But, I believe there is an alternative to assuming that the direction is simply random, because it appears they are constrained in a probabilistic sense. I proposed several years ago (Haith, 1973) that the system might work with something like "planned modules" such that a series of eye movements is predetermined in the sense that the movements satisfy certain constraints. That is, the specific location of each fixation might not be determined, but the constraints might be something like "stay near this edge and alternate direction of large eye movements for 3 seconds." This ISR command would, of course, be modulated by the activity of a suppressed ASR and would, no doubt, be interruptable by a significant peripheral event such as a light flash (which might reflect a kind of "stop" rule that the system obeys). Our best estimate of eye-movement reaction times in young infants (close to 1 second under the most ideal conditions) for babies who are 1-month-old, simply can not accommodate the fixation activity occurring at a rate of 2-3/second in newborns. To reiterate, I felt that I was studying the operation of an organized system and tried to discover the principles that it obeyed. "Reponses" and reflexes" and other terms that imply unitary behaviors play no role in this type of explanation.

A somewhat different set of issues concerns the notion of cortical-firing rates. Because of the established use of preference paradigms for studying infant vision, and because several theories of what controls infant preference or attention have been proposed, there is a tendency to believe that I am simply proposing that others have been wrong about the preference dimension they have proposed. This tendency would have me say, perhaps with others (for example, Karmel & Maisel, 1975), that babies, in fact, *prefer* high cortical-firing rates. Such rephrasing would seriously misrepresent my position. I feel preference interpretations are totally inappropriate. Thus, I also do not believe the baby strives for, or seeks, high cortical-firing rates, or "intends" to increase high cortical-firing rates. (I must admit the infant acts as though he/she does, and that some of my shorthand characterizations of the newborn might lead to this inference.) We can do very well without this type of anthropomorphizing by simply stating that the system is wired in such a way that maximizes firing. The system could operate on an ad hoc basis, each rule coming into play when appropriate. That is, given a certain firing rate by the ISR, the ASR manifests a given level of activity; if firing rate is low, ambient search increases and other, higher density, locales may be found. It is not that the baby looks around for stimuli with higher firing potential; the infant is simply wired to behave in a certain way given a certain set of circumstances. The baby need have no more knowledge of the consequences of his/her behavior than does a monkey who, out of fear, helps to warn his comrades of danger by incessant screaming. Thus, the rules do make sense because they correspond to what happens given certain situations; these rules "serve" the higher principles of increasing cortical-firing rate in a *system* sense.

It should be clear, then, that I make no claim that cortical-firing rate is "reinforcing," or that I accept any of the connotations implied by that term. First of all, there is no "behavior," in the sense of a response, to reinforce. In fact, there is even no scanning routine to reinforce. The baby is not *trying* to increase firing rate; rather, the infant behaves on an ad hoc basis (relatively speaking) with, usually, a resulting increase in cortical firing. But I would not be surprised to find short-term activities that decrease firing rate, nor would I be surprised to find the newborn looking more at low-density than high-density areas. When the ASR dominates activity because the ISR does not produce high enough firing, a relatively undirected scan occurs. Thus local areas of low-density contours could be found and scanned for a while. What this conceptualization does predict is how the baby will behave, on the average, and how the baby will scan portions of the array depending on the local contour density. The infant's behavior will be determined by the firing rate the ISR produces. Finally, I would claim that the ideas I proposed do not suffer from the circularity inherent in reinforcement interpretations. Aside from offering a very different way of thinking about visual activity, my notions refer to cortical activation—a measurable reality—not a construct that is definable in terms of the behavior it supposedly controls. In brief, activation or firing rate can be determined independently.

One last comment concerning the notion of firing rate: I have been asked repeatedly if I really mean that the newborn's actions are geared toward producing the highest possible firing rate. The suggestion is that perhaps the newborn actions can be understood in terms of maintenance of an *optimal* firing rate. I reject this possibility for two reasons. On the grounds of principle alone, I dislike optimal-level notions unless they are absolutely necessary, because they are virtually impossible to disprove and, thereby, have produced a great deal of trouble in psychology and especially in the field of infant vision. The problem is that a curvilinear function is usually assumed that peaks at some unknown value of a dimension. Additionally, the "optimal" level is thought to be different for each subject; if noncurvilinear functions are generated across levels of the crucial dimension, they can simply be attributed to failure to encompass values on both sides of the optimal level in the experiment. Virtually any function can be interpreted.

The second reason is that an optimal-level notion simply does not fit with the conceptualization I have proposed. Remember, the ISR suppresses the ASR to the extent that the ISR produces cortical firing. An asymptotic function fits this conception better; an asymptotic limit is expected because there must be a limit to how much the ASR can be suppressed. Thus, I suspect that the system operates to maximize firing rate up to some asymptotic limit. Concretely this would mean that *within the range of resolvable contour*—for example, increasing contour density would reduce scan dispersion up to some limit—and further density would produce no additional discernible effect.

It is perhaps possible to associate the ambient-scan routine with the second visual system and the inspection-scan routine with the primary visual systems, but I mean to imply no such relation. First of all, I am highly suspect of the dichotomy that has been proposed between these systems in the infant, as I have stated elsewhere (Haith & Campos, 1977, p. 260). Weiskrantz (1974) recently criticized the two-visual-system idea as too simplistic; recent neuroanatomical work has revealed a far more complicated set of structures and interconnections than originally believed. Additionally, the two systems that others have proposed have been described principally in *sensory* terms, less often in reflex terms, but not in terms of the *inspection* or *search* behaviors that we have been concerned with here. Of course, the sensory consequences of these inspection activities are important because the cortical firing resulting from these activities governs scanning activity.

Although I expect that net firing activity controls visual scanning to some extent throughout life, I suspect that it operates as a virtually exclusive control only within the first 6 weeks. After this time a variety of changes in visual behavior occurs: babies become sensitive to configurations (Cornell,

1975; Fantz et al., 1975; Ruff & Birch, 1974), learn visual contingencies and habituate to visual stimuli more easily (Jeffrey & Cohen, 1971; Kessen et al., 1970; Papousek, 1967), become sensitive to internal features of stimuli (Haith et al., 1977; Maurer & Salapatek, 1976; Milewski, 1976), and scan the visual array more extensively (Pipp, 1978; Pipp & Haith, 1977; Salapatek, 1975). Some of these findings could be interpreted by arguing that the asymptotic level of cortical firing at which maximum suppression of the ASR occurs increases with age. Or, one might argue that cortical-firing rate is controlled by different factors as the infant matures. However, my guess is that "tasks" other than maximizing cortical-firing rate assume higher importance and that the pattern rather than the absolute level of firing becomes crucial. Such "tasks" might include the synthesis of visual information, the search for contingencies and meaning, visual organization, and, generally, the variety of activities necessary to put a visual world of objects and spaces together.

I want to underline a final point in closing. I consider the arguments I have made regarding maximization of cortical-firing rates as the newborn's chief agenda item, to be speculative. Disconfirmation of this notion, from my point of view, would not destroy what I have attempted here, because that is not the major point. The major point is that a complete theory of visual activity must adopt an organism's point of view. The organization of that activity must be dealt with head-on and a stimulus-oriented theory is not adequate to the task. An adequate theory should address the adaptiveness of visual activity, its organization, the balance between stimulus-constrained and stimulus-unconstrained activity, the continuous activity inherent in visual behavior, and what makes the system go. I see little alternative to assuming that nature has set an agenda for the newborn, and, currently, no alternative theory accounts for as many facts as does the cortical-firing maximization position.

I hope future research will contribute to a more complete articulation of how the newborn visual system works and how the initial agenda of the newborn is modified to become the agenda(s) pursued by the older infant.

References

Alpern, M. Part I: Movements of the eyes. In H. Davson (Ed.),*The eye* (Vol. 3). New York: Academic Press, 1969.

Ames, E. W., & Silfen, C. K. *Methodological issues in the study of age differences in infants' attention to stimuli varying in movement and complexity.* Paper presented at the meeting of the Society for Research in Child Development, Minneapolis, March, 1965.

Annis, R. C., & Frost, B. Human visual ecology and orientation anistropies in acuity. *Science,* 1973, *182,* 729-731.

Anohkin, P. K. The multiple ascending influences of the subcortical centers on the cerebral cortex. In M.A.B. Brazier (Ed.), *Brain and behavior: Proceeding.* New York: Stechert, 1961.

Aslin, R. N., & Salapatek, P. *Saccadic localization of peripheral targets by the very young human infant.* Perception and Psychophysics, 1975, *17,* 293-302.

Barlow, H. B., Narasimhan, R., & Rosenfeld, A. Visual pattern analysis in machines and animals. *Science,* 1972, *177,* 567-575.

Barlow, H. B., & Pettigrew, J. D. Lack of specificity of neurons in the visual cortex of young kittens. *Journal of Physiology,* 1971, *218,* 98-100.

Barnet, A. B., Lodge, A., & Armington, J. C. Electroretinogram in newborn human infants. *Science,* 1965, *148,* 651-654.

Bender, M. B., & Shanzer, S. Oculomotor pathways defined by electric stimulation and lesions in the brainstem of the monkey. In M. B. Bender (Ed.), *The oculomotor system.* New York: Harper & Row, 1964.

Berlyne, D. E. The influence of the albedo and complexity of stimuli on visual fixation in the human infant. *British Journal of Psychology,* 1958, *49,* 315-318.

Berlyne, D. E. *Conflict, arousal, and curiosity.* New York: McGraw-Hill, 1960.

Blakemore, C., & Cooper, G. F. Development of the brain depends on visual environment. *Nature,* 1970, *228,* 472-478.

Blanton, M. G. The behavior of the human infant during the first thirty days of life. *Psychological Review,* 1917, *24,* 456-483.

Bond, E. Form perception in the infant. *Psychological Bulletin,* 1972, *77,* 225-245.

Brackbill, Y., Adams, G., Crowell, D. H., & Gray, M. L. Arousal level in neonates and preschool children under continuous auditory stimulation. *Journal of Experimental Child Psychology,* 1966, *4,* 178–188.

Brennan, W., Ames, E. W., & Moore, R. W. Age differences in infants' attention to patterns of different complexities. *Science,* 1966, *151,* 354–356.

Broadbent, D. E. Listening to one of the two synchronous messages. *Journal of Experimental Psychology,* 1952, *44,* 51–55.

Broadbent, D. E. *Perception and communication.* New York: Pergamon, 1958.

Bronson, G. The postnatal growth of visual capacity. *Child Development,* 1974, *45,* 873–890.

Bruner, J. S. *Processes of cognitive growth: Infancy.* Worcestor: Clark University Press, 1968.

Bruner, J. S., Goodnow, J. J., & Austin, G. A. *A study of thinking.* New York: Wiley, 1956.

Chase, W. P. Color vision in infants. *Journal of Experimental Psychology,* 1937, *20,* 203–222.

Clifton, R. K. Newborn heart-rate response and response habituation as a function of stimulus duration. *Journal of Experimental Child Psychology,* 1968, *6,* 265–278.

Cohen, L. B. Observing responses, visual preferences, and habituation to visual stimuli in infants. *Journal of Experimental Child Psychology,* 1969, *7,* 419–433.

Cohen, L. B., & Salapatek, P. *Infant perception.* New York: Academic Press, 1975.

Conel, J. L. The postnatal development of the human cerebral cortex. In *The cortex of the newborn* (Vol. 1). Cambridge: Harvard University Press, 1939.

Cornell, E. H. Infants' visual attention to pattern arrangement and orientation. *Child Development,* 1975, *46,* 229–232.

Cowey, A. The basis of a method of perimetry with monkeys. *Quarterly Journal of Experimental Psychology,* 1963, *15,* 81–90.

Crosby, E. C., Foss, R. E., & Henderson, J. W. The mammalian midbrain and isthmus regions. *Journal of Comparative Neurology,* 1952, *97,* 357–383.

Crosby, E. C., & Henderson, J. W. The mammalian midbrain and isthmus regions. Part II. Fiber connections of the superior colliculus. B. Pathways concerned in automatic eye movements. *Journal of Comparative Neurology,* 1948, *88,* 53–91.

Dayton, G. O., Jr., Jones, M. H., Aiu, P., Rawson, R. A., Steele, B., & Rose, M. Developmental study of coordinated eye movement in the human infant. I. Visual acuity in the newborn human: A study based on induced optokinetic nystagmus recorded by electrography. *Archives of Opthalmology,* 1964, *71,* 865–870.(a)

Dayton, G. O., Jr., Jones, M. H., Steele, B., & Rose, M. Developmental study of coordinated eye movements in the human infant. II. An electrooculographic study of the fixation reflex in the newborn. *Archives of Opthalmology,* 1964, *71,* 871–875.(b)

Dember, W. N., & Earl, R. W. Analysis of exploratory, manipulatory, and curiosity behaviors. *Psychological Review,* 1957, *64,* 91–96.

Dobson, V., & Teller, D. Y. Assessment of visual acuity in human infants. In J. Armington, J. Krauskopf, & B. Wooten (Eds.), *Visual psychophysics and Physiology: A volume dedicated to Lorrin Riggs,* New York: Academic Press, 1978.

Dodge, R. An experimental study of visual fixation. *Psychological Review,* 1907, *35,* 1–95.

Doris, J., Casper, M., & Poresky, R. Differential brightness thresholds in infancy. *Journal of Experimental Child Psychology,* 1967, *5,* 522–535.

Duffy, E. The psychological significance of the concept of "arousal" or "activation." *Psychological Review,* 1957, *64,* 265–275.

Duke-Elder, S., & Cook, C. *System of opthalmology (Vol. 3). Normal and abnormal development.* Part 1. *Embryology.* London: Henry Kimpton, 1963.

Ellingson, R. J. Cerebral electrical responses to auditory and visual stimuli in the infant (human and subhuman studies). In P. Kellaway & I. Petersen (Eds.), *Neurologic and electroencephalographic correlative studies in infancy.* New York: Grune & Stratton, 1964.

Fantz, R. L. Pattern vision in young infants. *Psychological Review,* 1958, *8,* 43–47.

Fantz, R. L. The origin of form perception. *Scientific American,* 1961, *204,* 66–72.

Fantz, R. L. Visual experience in infants: Decreased attention to familiar patterns relative to novel ones. *Science*, 1964, *146*, 668–670.

Fantz, R. L. Visual perception from birth as shown by pattern selectivity. *Annals of the New York Academcy of Science*, 1965, *118*, 793–814.

Fantz, R. L., Fagan, J. F., III, Miranda, S. B. Early visual selectivity. In L. B. Cohen & P. Salapatek (Eds.), *Infant perception: From sensation to cognition.* New York: Academic Press, 1975.

Fantz, R. L., & Nevis, S. Pattern preferences and perceptual-cognitive development in early infancy. *Merrill-Palmer Quarterly*, 1967, *13*, 77–108.

Fitts, P. M., Mizer, W., Rappaport, M., Anderson, N., & Leonard, J. A. Stimulus correlates of visual pattern recognition: A probability approach. *Journal of Experimental Psychology*, 1956, *51*, 1–11.

Freeman, R. D., Mitchell, D. E., & Millodot, M. A neural effect of partial visual deprivation in humans. *Science*, 1972, *175*, 1384–1386.

Freeman, R. D., & Thibos, L. W. Electrophysiological evidence that abnormal early visual experience can modify the human brain. *Science*, 1973, *180*, 876–878.

Friedman, S. Habituation and recovery of visual response in the alert human newborn. *Journal of Experimental Child Psychology*, 1972, *13*, 339–349.

Friedman, S., Bruno, L. A., & Vietze, P. Newborn habituation to visual stimuli: A sex difference in novelty detection. *Journal of Experimental Child Psychology*, 1974, *18*, 242–251.

Fuchs, A. F. The saccadic system. In P. Bach-y-Rita & C. C. Collins (Eds.), *The control of eye movement.* New York: Academic Press, 1971.

Gould, J. D. Looking at pictures. In R. A. Monty & J. W. Senders (Eds.), *Eye movements and psychological processes.* Hillsdale, N.J.: Lawrence Erlbaum Associates, 1976.

Graham, F. K., & Jackson, J. C. Arousal systems and infant heart rate responses. In H. W. Reese & L. P. Lipsitt (Eds.), *Advances in child development and behavior* (Vol. 5). New York: Academic Press, 1970.

Haaf, R. A., & Bell, R. Q. A facial dimension in visual discrimination by human infants. *Child Development*, 1967, *38*, 893–899.

Haber, R. N., & Hershenson, M. *The psychology of visual perception.* New York: Holt, Rinehart & Winston, 1973.

Haith, M. M. The response of the human newborn to visual movement. *Journal of Experimental Child Psychology*, 1966, *3*, 235–243.

Haith, M. M. Infrared television recording and measurement of ocular behavior in the human infant. *American Psychologist*, 1969, *24*, 279–283.

Haith, M. M. Visual scanning in infants. Paper presented at the regional meeting of the Society for Research in Child Development, Clark University, 1968. In L. J. Stone, H. T. Smith, & R. B. Murphy (Eds.), *The competent infant: A handbook of readings.* New York: Basic Books, 1973.

Haith, M. M. Visual competence in early infancy. In R. Held, H. Leibowitz, & H. L. Teuber (Eds.), *Handbook of sensory physiology* (VIII). Berlin: Springer-Verlag, 1978.

Haith, M. M., Bergman, T., & Moore, M. J. Eye contact and face scanning in early infancy. *Science*, 1977, *198*, 853–855.

Haith, M., & Campos, J. Human infancy. *Annual Review of Psychology*, 1977, *28*, 251–293.

Haith, M. M., Kessen, W., & Collins, D. Response of the human infant to level of complexity of intermittent visual movement. *Journal of Experimental Child Psychology*, 1969, *7*, 52–69.

Harrington, D. O. *The visual fields.* London: Henry Kimpton, 1964.

Harris, P., & MacFarlane, A. The growth of the effective visual field from birth to seven weeks. *Journal of Experimental Child Psychology*, 1974, *18*, 340–348.

Hartline, H. K. The response of single optic nerve fibers of the vertebrate eye to illumination of the retina. *American Journal of Physiology*, 1938, *121*, 400–415.

Hartline, H. K. Visual receptors and retinal interaction. *Science,* 1969, *164,* 270-278.

Haynes, H., White, B. L., & Held, R. Visual accommodation in human infants. *Science,* 1965, *148,* 528-530.

Hebb, D. O. *Organization of behavior.* New York: Wiley, 1949.

Hershenson, M. Visual discrimination in the human newborn. *Journal of Comparative Physiology and Psychology,* 1964, *58,* 270-276.

Hershenson, M. Development of the perception of form. *Psychological Bulletin,* 1967, *58,* 326-336.

Hershenson, M. The development of visual perceptual systems. In H. Moltz (Ed.), *The ontogeny of vertebrate behavior.* New York: Academic Press, 1970.

Hershenson, M., Munsinger, H., & Kessen, W. Preference for shapes of intermediate variability in the newborn human. *Science,* 1965, *147,* 630-631.

Hirsch, H., & Spinelli, N. Distribution of receptive field orientation: Modification contingent on conditions of visual experience. *Science,* 1970, *168,* 869-871.

Horowitz, F. D. Infant learning and development: Retrospect and prospect. *Merrill-Palmer Quarterly,* 1968, *14,* 101-120.

Horowitz, F. D., Paden, L. Y., Bhana, K., & Self, P. A. An infant-control procedure for studying infant visual fixations. *Developmental Psychology,* 1972, *7,* 90.

Horsten, G. P., & Winkelman, J. E. Electrical activity of the retina in relation to histological differentiation in infants born prematurely and at full term. *Vision Research,* 1962, *2,* 269-276.

Horsten, G. P., & Winkelman, J. E. Electro-retinographic critical fusion frequency of the retina in relation to the histological development in man and animals. *Ophthalmologica,* 1964, *18,* 515-521.

Hubel, D. H., & Wiesel, T. N. Receptive fields of single neurons in the cat's striate cortex. *Journal of Physiology,* 1959, *148,* 574-591.

Hubel, D. H., & Wiesel, T. N. Receptive fields, binocular interaction and functional architecture in the cat's visual cortex. *Journal of Physiology,* 1962, *160,* 106-154.

Hubel, D. H., & Wiesel, T. N. Receptive fields of cells in striate cortex of very young visually inexperienced kittens. *Journal of Neurophysiology,* 1963, *26,* 944-1002.

Hubel, D. H., & Wiesel, T. N. Receptive fields and functional architecture of monkey striate cortex. *Journal of Physiology,* 1968, *195,* 215-243.

Irwin, O. C., & Weiss, L. A. The effect of darkness on the activity of newborn infants. *University of Iowa Studies on Child Welfare,* 1934, *9,* 163-175.

James, W. *The principles of psychology.* New York: Henry Holt, 1890.

Jeffrey, W. E. The orienting reflex and attention in cognitive development. *Psychological Review,* 1968, *75,* 323-334.

Jeffrey, W. E., & Cohen, L. B. Habituation in the human infant. In H. Reese (Ed.), *Advances in child development and behavior* (Vol. 6). New York: Academic Press, 1971.

Jones, M. C. The development of early behavior patterns in young children. *Pedagogical Seminary,* 1926, *33,* 537-585.

Kagan, J. Attention and psychological change in the young child. *Science,* 1970, *170,* 826-832.

Karmel, B. Z. The effects of age, complexity, and amount of contour on pattern preferences in human infants. *Journal of Experimental Child Psychology,* 1969, *7,* 339-354.

Karmel, B. Z., & Maisel, E. B. A neuronal activity model for infant visual attention. In L. B. Cohen & P. Salapatek (Eds.), *Infant perception from sensation to cognition. Part 1. Basic visual processes* (Vol. 1). New York: Academic Press, 1975.

Kearsley, R. The newborn's response to auditory stimulation: A demonstration of orienting and reflexive behavior. *Child Development,* 1973, *44,* 582-590.

Kessen, W. *The construction of form.* Paper presented at the meeting of the New England Psychological Association, Boston, October 1966.

Kessen, W., Haith, M. M., & Salapatek, P. Human infancy: A bibliography and guide. In P. Mussen (Ed.), *Carmichael's manual of child psychology.* New York: Wiley, 1970.

Kessen, W., Salapatek, P., & Haith, M. M. The visual response of the newborn to linear contour. *Journal of Experimental Child Psychology,* 1972, *13,* 9–20.

Komoda, M. K., Festinger, L., Phillips, L. J., Duckman, R. H., & Young, R. A. Some observations concerning saccadic eye movements. *Vision Research,* 1973, *13,* 1009–1020.

Kron, R. E., Stein, M., & Goddard, K. E. Newborn sucking behavior affected by obstetric sedation. *Pediatrics,* 1966, *37,* 1012–1016.

Kuffler, S. W. Discharge patterns and functional organization of mammalian retina. *Journal of Neurophysiology,* 1953, *16,* 37–68.

Lentz, R., & Haith, M. M. Audio tape storage of experimental data: An application to tachistoscopic research with children. *Behavior Research Methods and Instrumentation.* 1969, *1,* 273–275.

Lewis, M. Infant's responses to facial stimuli during the first year of life. *Developmental Psychology,* 1969, *1,* 75–86.

Maffei, L., & Campbell, F. W. Neurophysiological localization of the vertical and horizontal visual coordinates in man. *Science,* 1970, *167,* 386–387.

Mann, I. *The development of the human eye.* London: British Medical Assocation, 1964.

Maurer, D., & Salapatek, P. Developmental changes in the scanning of faces by infants. *Child Development,* 1976, *47,* 523–527.

McCall, R. B., & Kagan, J. Attention in the infant: Effects of complexity, contour, perimeter, and familiarity. *Child Development,* 1967, *38,* 939–952.

McCall, R. B., Kennedy, C. B., & Appelbaum, J. I. Magnitude of discrepancy and the distribution of attention in infants. *Child Development,* 1977, *48,* 772–785.

McCall, R. B., & Melson, W. H. Complexity, contour, and area as determinants of attention in infants. *Developmental Psychology,* 1970, *3,* 343–349.

McGinnis, J. M. Eye movements and optic nystagmus in early infancy. *Genetic Psychology Monographs,* 1930, *8,* 321–430.

Mendelson, M. J., & Haith, M. M. The relation between nonnutritive sucking and visual information processing in the human newborn. *Child Development,* 1975, *46,* 1025–1029.

Mendelson, M. J., & Haith, M. M. The relation between audition and vision in the human newborn. *Monographs of the Society for Research in Child Development,* 1976, *41,* 1–61.

Mettler, F. A. Supratentorial mechanisms influencing the oculomotor apparatus. In M. B. Bender (Ed.), *The oculomotor system.* New York: Harper & Row, 1964.

Milewski, A. Infant's discrimination of internal and external pattern elements. *Journal of Experimental Psychology,* 1976, *22,* 229–246.

Miller, G. A., Galanter, E., & Pribram, K. H. *Plans and the structure of behavior.* New York: Holt, Rinehart & Winston, 1960.

Mize, R. R., & Murphy, E. H. Selective visual experience fails to modify receptive field properties of rabbit striate cortex. *Science,* 1973, *180,* 320–322.

Moffett, A. Stimulus complexity as a determinant of visual attention in infants. *Journal of Experimental Child Psychology,* 1969, *8,* 173–179.

Nelson, K., & Kessen, W. *Visual scanning by human newborns: Responses to complete triangle, to sides only, and to corners only.* Paper presented at the meeting of the American Psychological Association, September, 1969.

Noda, H., Freeman, R. B., & Creutzfeldt, O. O. Neuronal correlates of eye movements in the visual cortex of the cat. *Science,* 1972, *175,* 661–664.

Ordy, J. M., Samorajski, T., Collins, R. L., & Nagy, A. R. Postnatal development of vision in a subhuman primate (Macacca Mulatta). *Archives of Ophthalmology,* 1965, *73,* 674–686.

Paden, L. Y. The effects of variations of auditory stimulation (music) and interspersed stimulus procedures on visual attending behavior in infants. In F. Horowitz (Ed.), *Monographs of the Society for Research in Child Development,* 1975, *39,* 29–41.

Papousek, H. Experimental studies of appetitional behavior in human newborns and infants. In H. W. Stevenson, E. H. Hess, & H. L. Rheingold (Eds.), *Early behavior.* New York: Wiley, 1967.

Pasik, P., & Pasik, T. Oculomotor functions in monkeys with lesions of the cerebrum and the superior colliculi. In M. B. Bender (Ed.), *The oculomotor system.* New York: Harper & Row, 1964.

Peiper, A. *Cerebral function in infancy and childhood.* New York: Consultants Bureau, 1963.

Pettigrew, J. D. The effect of visual experience on the development of stimulus specificity by kitten cortical neurons. *Journal of Physiology,* 1974, *237,* 49–74.

Pettigrew, J. D., & Freeman, R. D. Visual experience without lines: Effect on developing cortical neurons. *Science,* 1973, *182,* 599–601.

Piaget, J. *The origins of intelligence in children.* New York: Norton, 1951.

Pipp, S. A test of theories of infant visual perception in the first two months of life. Unpublished doctoral dissertation. University of Denver, 1978.

Pipp, S., & Haith, M. M. Infant visual scanning of two- and three-dimensional forms. *Child Development,* 1977, *48,* 1640–1644.

Pratt, K. C. The neonate. In L. Carmichael (Ed.), *Manual of child psychology.* New York: Wiley, 1954.

Pratt, K. C., Nelson, A. K., & Sun, K. H. The behavior of the newborn infant. Ohio State University Studies, *Contributions in Psychology,* 1930, No. 10.

Purpura, D. P. Morphophysiological basis of elementary evoked response patterns in the neocortex of the newborn cat. Pavlovian Conference on High Neuron Activity. *Annals of the New York Academy of Science,* 1961, *92,* 840–859.

Purpura, D. P. Synaptogenesis in mammalian cortex: Problems and perspectives. In M. B. Sterman, D. J. McGinty, & A. M. Adinolfi (Eds.), *Brain development and behavior.* New York: Academic Press, 1971.

Rakic, P. Neurons in rhesus monkey visual cortex: Systematic relation between time of origin and eventual disposition. *Science,* 1974, *183,* 425–427.

Ratliff, F. Inhibitory interaction and the detection and enhancement of contours. In W. A. Rosenblith (Ed.), *Sensory Communication.* Cambridge: MIT Press, 1961.

Ratliff, F. *Mach bonds: Quantitative studies on neural networks in the retina.* San Francisco: Holden-Day, 1965.

Ratliff, F., & Hartline, H. K. The responses of *Limulus* optic nerve fibers to patterns of illumination on the receptor mosaic. *Journal of General Physiology,* 1959, *42,* 1241–1255.

Robinson, D. A. Oculomotor unit behavior in the monkey. *Journal of Neurophysiology,* 1970, *33,* 393–404.

Robinson, D. A., & Fuchs, A. F. Eye movements evoked by stimulation of frontal eye fields. *Journal of Neurophysiology,* 1969, *32,* 637–648.

Roffwarg, H. P., Muzio, J. N., & Dement, W. C. Ontogenetic development of the human sleep-dream cycle. *Science,* 1966, *152,* 604–619.

Rose, G., & Ellingson, R. J. Ontogenesis of evoked potentials. In W. A. Himwich (Ed.), *Developmental neurobiology.* Springfield, Ill.: Charles C. Thomas, 1970.

Rose, G. H. Relationship of electrophysiological and behavioral indices of visual development of mammals. In M. B. Sterman, D. J. McGinty, & A. M. Adinolfi (Eds.), *Brain development and behavior.* New York: Academic Press, 1971.

Rose, G. H., & Lindsley, D. B. Development of visually evoked potentials in kittens: Specific and non-specific responses. *Journal of Neurophysiology,* 1968, *31,* 607–623.

Ruff, H. A., & Birch, H. G. Infant visual fixation: The effect of concentricity, curvilinearity, and number of directions. *Journal of Experimental Child Psychology,* 1974, *17,* 460–473.

Salapatek, P. Visual scanning of geometric figures by the human newborn. *Journal of Comparative Physiology and Psychology,* 1968, *66,* 247–258.

Salapatek, P. Pattern perception in early infancy. In L. B. Cohen & P. Salapatek (Eds.), *Infant perception: From sensation to cognition.* New York: Academic Press, 1975.

Salapatek, P., Haith, M. M., Maurer, D., & Kessen, W. Error in the corneal-reflection technique: A note on Slater and Findlay. *Journal of Experimental Child Psychology,* 1972, *14,* 493–497.

Salapatek, P., & Kessen, W. Visual scanning of triangles by the human newborn. *Journal of Experimental Child Psychology,* 1966, *3,* 155–167.

Salk, L. The effects of the normal heartbeat sound on the behavior of the newborn infant: Implications for mental health. *World Mental Health,* 1960, *12,* 168–175.

Salk, L. The importance of the heartbeat rhythm to human nature: Theoretical, clinical and experimental observations. In Proceedings of the 3rd World Congress on Psychiatry, (Vol. 1). Montreal: McGill University Press, 1961.

Salk, L. Mother's heartbeat as an imprinting stimulus. *Transactions of the New York Academcy of Science,* 1962, *24,* 753–763.

Scheibel, A. B. Neural correlates of psychophysiological development in the young organism. In J. Wortis (Ed.), *Recent advances in biological psychiatry* (Vol. 4). New York: Plenum, 1962.

Scheibel, M. E., & Scheibel, A. B. Neural correlates of psychophysiological development in the young organism. *Anatomical Record,* 1961, *139,* 319–320.

Sharpless, A., & Jasper, H. Habituation of the arousal reaction. *Brain,* 1956, *79,* 655–680.

Slater, A. M., & Findlay, J. M. The measurement of fixation position in the newborn baby. *Journal of Experimental Child Psychology,* 1972, *14,* 349–364.

Sokolov, E. N. *Perception and the conditioned reflex.* New York: MacMillan, 1960.

Stark, L. The control system for versional eye movements. In P. Bach-y-Rita & C. C. Collins (Eds.), *The control of eye movements.* New York: Academic Press, 1971.

Stechler, G., & Latz, E. Some observations on attention and arousal in the human infant. *Journal of the American Academy of Child Psychiatry,* 1966, *5,* 517–525.

Stirnimann, F. Uber das Farbempfinden Neugeborener. *Annales Paediatrici,* 1944, *163,* 1–25.

Thomas, H. Visual-fixation responses of infants to stimuli of varying complexity. *Child Development,* 1965, *36,* 629–638.

Thomas, H. Unfolding the baby's mind: The infant's selection of visual stimuli. *Psychological Review,* 1973, *80,* 468–488.

Volkmann, F. C. Vision during voluntary saccadic eye movements. *Journal of the Optical Society of America,* 1962, *52,* 571–578.

Volkmann, F. C., Schick, A. M. L., & Riggs, L. A. Time course of visual inhibition during voluntary saccades. *Journal of the Optical Society of America,* 1968, *58,* 562–569.

Von Bertalanffy, L. *General systems theory.* New York: Braziller, 1968.

Wagman, S. H. Eye movements induced by electric stimulation of cerebrum in monkeys and their relationship to bodily movement. In M. B. Bender (Ed.), *The oculomotor system.* New York: Harper & Row, 1964.

Warren, R. M., & Warren, R. P. *Helmholtz on perception: Its physiology and development.* New York: Wiley, 1968.

Weiskrantz, L. The interaction between occipital and temporal cortex in vision: An overview. In F. O. Schmitt & F. G. Worden (Eds.), *The neurosciences third study program.* Cambridge: MIT Press, 1974.

Weiss, L. A. Differential reactions of newborn infants to different degrees of light intensity. *Proceedings of the Iowa Academy of Science,* 1933, *40,* 198–199.

Weiss, L. A. Differential variations in the amount of activity of newborn infants under controlled light and sound stimulation. *University of Iowa Studies on Child Welfare,* 1934, *9,* 9–74.

Westheimer, G. Eye movement responses to a horizontally moving visual stimulus. *Archives of Ophthalmology,* 1954, *52,* 932–941.

Wickelgren, L. W. Convergence in the human newborn. *Journal of Experimental Child Psychology,* 1967, *5,* 74–85.

Wiesel, T. N., & Hubel, D. H. Ordered arrangement of orientation columns in monkeys lacking visual experience. *Journal of Comparative Neurology,* 1974, *158,* 307–318.

Wilcox, B. M. Visual preferences of human infants for representations of the human face. *Journal of Experimental Child Psychology,* 1969, *7,* 10–20.

Wilson, M. E., & Toyne, M. J. Retinotectal and cortico-tectal projections in Macacca Mulatta. *Brain Research,* 1970, *24,* 395–406.

Wilson, P. D., & Riesen, A. Monkeys deprived of patterned light. *Journal of Comparative Physiology and Psychology,* 1966, *61,* 87–95.

Wohlwill, J. F., & Wiener, M. Discrimination of form orientation in young children. *Child Development,* 1964, *35,* 1113–1125.

Wolff, P. H. Observations on newborn infants. *Psychosomatic Medicine,* 1959, *21,* 110–118.

Wurtz, R. H. Visual cortex neurons: Response to stimuli during rapid eye movements. *Science,* 1968, *162,* 1148–1150.

Wyckoff, L. B. The role of observing responses in discrimination learning. Part I. *Psychological Review,* 1952, *59,* 431–442.

Zelazo, P. R., Hopkins, J. R., Jacobson, S., & Kagan, J. Psychological reactivity to discrepant events. *International Journal of Cognitive Psychology,* 1974, *2,* 385–393.

Zetterström, B. The clinical electroretinogram: IV. The electroretinogram in children during the first year of life. *Acta Ophthalmologica,* 1951, *29,* 295–304.

Zetterström, B. Flicker electroretinography in newborn infants. *Acta Ophthalmologica,* 1955, *33,* 157–166.

Author Index

139

Subject Index